MCSE Test Success:
TCP/IP for NT 4

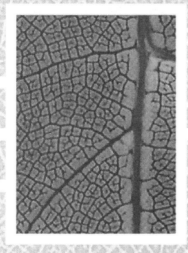

MCSE Test Success™:
TCP/IP for NT® 4

VFX Technologies, Inc.

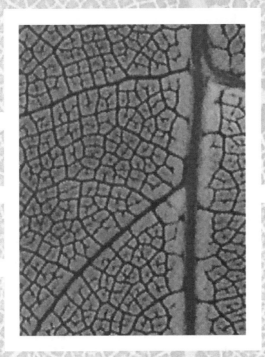

NETWORK PRESS ®
SYBEX

San Francisco • Paris • Düsseldorf • Soest

Associate Publisher: Guy Hart-Davis
Contracts and Licensing Manager: Kristine Plachy
Acquisitions & Developmental Editor: Bonnie Bills
Editor: Pat Coleman
Project Editor: Dann McDorman
Technical Editor: Jim Cooper
Book Designers: Patrick Dintino, Bill Gibson
Graphic Illustrator: Michael Gushard
Electronic Publishing Specialist: Bill Gibson
Production Coordinator: Eryn L. Osterhaus
Indexer: Ted Laux
Cover Designer: Archer Design
Cover Illustrator/Photographer: FPG International

Screen reproductions produced with Collage Complete.

Collage Complete is a trademark of Inner Media Inc.

SYBEX, Network Press, and the Network Press logo are registered trademarks of SYBEX Inc.

Test Success is a trademark of SYBEX Inc.

TRADEMARKS: SYBEX has attempted throughout this book to distinguish proprietary trademarks from descriptive terms by following the capitalization style used by the manufacturer.

Microsoft® Internet Explorer ©1996 Microsoft Corporation. All rights reserved. Microsoft, the Microsoft Internet Explorer logo, Windows, Windows NT, and the Windows logo are either registered trademarks or trademarks of Microsoft Corporation in the United States and/or other countries.

The author and publisher have made their best efforts to prepare this book, and the content is based upon final release software whenever possible. Portions of the manuscript may be based upon pre-release versions supplied by software manufacturer(s). The author and the publisher make no representation or warranties of any kind with regard to the completeness or accuracy of the contents herein and accept no liability of any kind including but not limited to performance, merchantability, fitness for any particular purpose, or any losses or damages of any kind caused or alleged to be caused directly or indirectly from this book.

SYBEX is an independent entity from Microsoft Corporation, and not affiliated with Microsoft Corporation in any manner. This publication may be used in assisting students to prepare for a Microsoft Certified Professional Exam. Neither Microsoft Corporation, its designated review company, nor SYBEX warrants that use of this publication will ensure passing the relevant exam. Microsoft is either a registered trademark or trademark of Microsoft Corporation in the United States and/or other countries.

Library of Congress Card Number: 98-85462
ISBN: 0-7821-2251-5

Manufactured in the United States of America

10 9 8 7 6 5 4 3 2 1

November 1, 1997

Dear SYBEX Customer:

Microsoft is pleased to inform you that SYBEX is a participant in the Microsoft® Independent Courseware Vendor (ICV) program. Microsoft ICVs design, develop, and market self-paced courseware, books, and other products that support Microsoft software and the Microsoft Certified Professional (MCP) program.

To be accepted into the Microsoft ICV program, an ICV must meet set criteria. In addition, Microsoft reviews and approves each ICV training product before permission is granted to use the Microsoft Certified Professional Approved Study Guide logo on that product. This logo assures the consumer that the product has passed the following Microsoft standards:

- The course contains accurate product information.
- The course includes labs and activities during which the student can apply knowledge and skills learned from the course.
- The course teaches skills that help prepare the student to take corresponding MCP exams.

Microsoft ICVs continually develop and release new MCP Approved Study Guides. To prepare for a particular Microsoft certification exam, a student may choose one or more single, self-paced training courses or a series of training courses.

You will be pleased with the quality and effectiveness of the MCP Approved Study Guides available from SYBEX.

Sincerely,

Holly Heath
ICV Account Manager
Microsoft Training & Certification

MICROSOFT INDEPENDENT COURSEWARE VENDOR PROGRAM

Acknowledgments

The author is only one of the people involved in creating a book. I'd like thank my family (both human and feline) for their support while I was working on this project. (Well, Scott, the human part of the family, was supportive. The three feline members tried to sleep on the keyboard while I was working and had to be restrained.) I'd also like to thank the crew at Sybex for their suggestions on how to make this book even better, particularly Bonnie Bills, Dann McDorman, Pat Coleman, Jim Cooper, Bill Gibson, and Eryn L. Osterhaus. And finally, thanks to Doug Archell for putting me in touch with Sybex for this project in the first place.

Christa Anderson

Contents at a Glance

Table of Contents

Introduction

One of the greatest challenges facing corporate America today is finding people who are qualified to manage corporate computer networks. Many companies have Microsoft networks, which run Windows 95, Windows NT, and other Microsoft BackOffice products (such as Microsoft SQL Server and Systems Management Server).

Microsoft developed its Microsoft certification program to certify those people who have the skills to work with Microsoft products and networks. The most highly coveted certification is MCSE, or Microsoft Certified Systems Engineer.

Why become an MCSE? Knowlege is important, but the MCSE can also gain a more tangible benefit: money. You will have much greater earning potential with this certification, as an MCSE carries high industry recognition. Certification can be your key to a new job or a higher salary—or both.

So what's stopping you? If it's because you don't know what to expect from the tests or are worried that you might not pass, this book is for you.

Your Key to Passing Exam 70-059

This book provides you with the key to passing Exam 70-059, Internetworking with Microsoft TCP/IP on Windows NT 4.0. Inside, you'll find all the information relevant to this exam, including hundreds of practice questions designed to make sure that you're ready for even the picky questions about less frequently used options.

Understand the Exam Objectives

To help you prepare for certification exams, Microsoft provides a list of objectives for each test. This book is structured according to the objectives for Exam 70-059, which measure your ability to design, administer, and troubleshoot TCP/IP networks under Windows NT 4.

At-a-glance review sections and hundreds of study questions bolster your knowledge of the information relevant to each objective and the exam itself. You learn exactly what you need to know without wasting time on background material or detailed explanations.

This book provides a final review of the information you'll need to pass the exam, although to be ready for the real world, you need to study the subject in greater depth and get a good deal of hands-on practice.

Get Ready for the Real Thing

More than 150 sample test questions prepare you for the test-taking experience. These are multiple-choice questions that resemble actual exam questions—some are even more difficult than what you'll find on the exam. If you can pass the Sample Tests at the end of each unit and the Final Review in Unit 6, you'll know you're ready.

Is This Book for You?

This book is intended for those who already have some experience with TCP/IP. It is especially well suited for:

- Students using courseware or taking a class to prepare for the exam, and who need to supplement their study material with test-based practice questions.

- Network engineers who have worked with TCP/IP but want to make sure there are no gaps in their knowledge.

- Anyone who has studied for the exams—by using self-study guides, by participating in computer-based training or classes, or by getting on-the-job experience—and wants to make sure that they're adequately prepared.

Understanding Microsoft Certification

Microsoft offers several levels of certification for anyone who has or is pursuing a career as a network professional working with Microsoft products:

- Microsoft Certified Professional (MCP)

- Microsoft Certified Systems Engineer (MCSE)

- Microsoft Certified Professional + Internet

- Microsoft Certified Systems Engineer + Internet

- Microsoft Certified Trainer (MCT)

The level you choose depends on your area of expertise and your career goals.

Microsoft Certified Professional (MCP)

This certification is for individuals with expertise in one specific area. MCP certification is often a stepping stone to MCSE certification and allows you some benefits of Microsoft certification after just one exam.

By passing one core exam (meaning an operating system exam), you become an MCP.

Microsoft Certified Systems Engineer (MCSE)

For network professionals, the MCSE certification requires commitment. You need to complete all the steps required for certification. Passing the exams shows that you meet the high standards that Microsoft has set for MCSEs.To become an MCSE, you must pass a series of six exams:

1. Networking Essentials (waived for Novell CNEs) (70-058)

2. Either Implementing and Supporting Microsoft Windows 95 (70-064) or Windows NT Workstation 4.0 (70-073)

3. Implementing and Supporting Microsoft Windows NT Server 4.0 (70-067)

4. Implementing and Supporting Microsoft Windows NT Server 4.0 in the Enterprise (70-068)

5. Elective

6. Elective

Some of the electives include:

- Internetworking with Microsoft TCP/IP on Microsoft Windows NT 4.0 (70-059)

- Implementing and Supporting Microsoft Internet Information Server 4.0 (70-087)

- Implementing and Supporting Microsoft Proxy Server v2.0 (70-088)

- Implementing and Supporting Microsoft Exchange Server 5.5 (70-081)

- Implementing and Supporting Microsoft SNA Server 4.0 (70-085)

- Implementing and Supporting Microsoft Systems Management Server 1.2 (70-018)

- Implementing a Database Design on Microsoft SQL Server 6.5 (70-027)

- System Administration for Microsoft SQL Server 6.5 (70-026)

For fast access to a complete list of all Microsoft certification exams and links to their exam-specific pages, go to http://www.microsoft.com/train_cert/html/exam.htm.

Microsoft Certified Trainer (MCT)

As an MCT, you can deliver Microsoft certified courseware through official Microsoft channels.

The MCT certification is more costly than the other options, because in addition to passing the exams, it requires that you sit through the official Microsoft courses. You also need to submit an application to be approved by Microsoft. The number of exams you are required to pass depends on the number of courses you want to teach.

Preparing for the MCSE Exams

To prepare for the MCSE certification exams, you should try to work with the product as much as possible. In addition, you can learn about the products and exams from a variety of resources:

- You can take instructor-led courses.

- Online training is an alternative to instructor-led courses. This is a useful option for people who cannot find any courses in their area or who do not have the time to attend classes.

- If you prefer to use a book to help you prepare for the MCSE tests, you can choose from a wide variety of publications. These range from complete study guides (such as the Network Press *MCSE Study Guide* series, which covers the core MCSE exams and key electives) through test-preparedness books similar to this one.

After you complete your courses, training, or study guides, you'll find the *MCSE Test Success* books an excellent resource for preparing you for the test. You will discover if you've got it covered or if you still need to fill some holes.

For more MCSE information, point your browser to the Sybex Web site, where you'll find information about the MCP program, job links, and descriptions of other quality titles in the Network Press line of MCSE-related books. Go to http://www.sybex.com/ and click on the MCSE logo.

Scheduling and Taking an Exam

Once you think you are ready to take an exam, call Sylvan Prometric Testing Centers at (800) 755-EXAM (800/755-3926). They'll tell you where to find the closest testing center. Before you call, get out your credit card; each exam costs $100.

You can schedule the exam for a time convenient for you. The exams are downloaded from Sylvan Prometric to the testing center, and you show up at your scheduled time and take the exam on a computer.

Once you complete the exam, you will know right away whether you have passed. At the end of the exam, you will receive a score report. It will list the six areas you were tested on and how you performed. If you pass the exam, you don't need to do anything else—Sylvan Prometric uploads the test results to Microsoft. If you don't pass, it's another $100 to schedule the exam again. But at least you will know from the score report where you did poorly, and you can study the areas in which you need work.

You can also register online. To do so, go to http://www.prometric.com/testingcandidates/register/reg.asp.

Test-Taking Hints

If you know what to expect, your chances of passing the exam will be much greater. Here are some tips that can help you achieve success.

Get there early and be prepared This is your last chance to review. Bring your *MCSE Test Success* book and review any areas with which you are not comfortable.

If you need a quick drink of water or a visit to the restroom, take the time before the exam. Once your exam starts, it will not be paused for these needs.

When you arrive for your exam, you will be asked to present two forms of identification, one with a signature. You will also be asked to sign a piece of paper verifying that you understand the testing rules (for example, the rule that says you will not cheat on the exam).

Before you start the exam, you will have an opportunity to take a practice exam. It is not related to Windows 95 and is simply offered so you will have a feel for the exam process.

You can't take it with you These are closed-book exams. Many testing centers are very strict about what you can take into the testing room. Although the exact security requirements seem to depend on the individual testing center, some centers even forbid you to bring in items such as a zipped-up purse.

The testing center will provide you with scratch paper. Use this paper as much as possible to diagram the questions. Many times diagramming questions will help make the answer clear. You will have to give this paper back to the test administrator at the end of the exam.

If you feel tempted to take in any outside material, be aware that many testing centers use monitoring devices such as video and audio equipment. Prometric Testing Centers take the test-taking process and the test validation very seriously.

Test approach   As you take the test, if you know the answer to a question, fill it in and move on. If you're not sure of the answer, mark your best guess, and then "mark" the question so that at the end of the exam you can review the questions you marked and check your answers.

At the end of the exam, you can review the questions. Depending on the amount of time remaining, you can then view all of the questions again, or you can view only the questions that you "marked." I always like to double-check all of my answers, just in case I misread any of the questions on the first pass. (Sometimes half the battle is in trying to figure out exactly what the question is asking you.) Also, sometimes I find that a related question later in the exam provides a clue for a question about which I was uncertain.

Read carefully, as the questions seem to be phrased to be confusing on purpose. This is not the time to skim!

Remember: Answer all the questions. Unanswered questions are scored as incorrect and will count against you. Also, be sure you keep an eye on the remaining time so you can pace yourself accordingly.

Don't worry if you don't own a watch. The upper right corner of your testing monitor will display both the current time and the number of minutes you have left.

If you do not pass the exam, note everything you can remember while the exam is still fresh in your mind. This will help you prepare for your next try. Although the next exam will not be exactly the same, the questions will be similar, and you don't want to make the same mistakes.

After You Become Certified

Once you become an MCSE, Microsoft kicks in some goodies, including:

- A one-year subscription to Microsoft TechNet, a monthly CD that contain Microsoft support information (including online versions of all product resource kits), service packs, utilities, and driver updates.

- A one-year subscription to the Microsoft Beta Evaluation program, which is a great way to get your hands on new software. Be the first kid on the block to play with new and upcoming operating systems and evaluations.

- Access to a secured area of the Microsoft Web site that provides technical support and product information. This certification benefit is also available for MCP certification.

- Permission to use the Microsoft Certified Professional logos (each certification has its own logo), which look great on letterhead and business cards.

- A certificate (you will get a certificate for each level of certification you reach).

- A one-year subscription to *Microsoft Certified Professional Magazine*, which provides information on professional and career development.

How to Use This Book

This book is designed to help you prepare for the MCSE exam. It reviews each objective and relevant test-taking information and offers you a chance to test your knowledge through study questions and sample tests.

The first five units in this book correspond to the Microsoft objectives groupings:

- Planning

- Installation and Configuration

- Connectivity

- Monitoring and Optimization

- Troubleshooting

The sixth unit is the Final Review, which contains test questions pertaining to all the previous units.

For each unit:

1. Review the exam objectives at the beginning of the unit. (You may want to check the Microsoft Training Certification Web site at http://www.microsoft.com/Train_Cert/ to make sure the objectives haven't changed, as they're updated fairly often.)

2. Read through or scan the reference material that follows the objectives list. Broken down according to the objectives, this section helps you brush up on the information you need to know for the exam.

3. Review your knowledge in the Study Questions section. These are straightforward questions designed to test your knowledge of the specific topic. Answers to Study Questions are in the appendix at the back of the book.

4. Once you feel sure of your knowledge of the area, take the Sample Test at the end of the unit. The Sample Test's content and style matches the real exam. Set yourself a time limit based on the number of questions.

The general rule of thumb is that you should be able to answer 20 questions in 30 minutes.

When you've finished, check your answers with the appendix in the back of the book. If you answer at least 85 percent of the questions correctly within the time limit the first time you take each Sample Test, you're in good shape. To really prepare, you should note the questions you miss and be able to score 95 to 100 percent correctly on subsequent tries.

After you successfully complete Units 1–5, take the Final Review in Unit 6. Allow yourself 100 minutes to complete the test. If you answer 85 percent of the questions correctly on the first try, you're well prepared. If not, go back and review your knowledge of the areas you struggled with, and take the test again.

Right before you take the test, scan the reference material at the beginning of each unit to refresh your memory.

At this point, you are well on your way to becoming certified. Good luck!

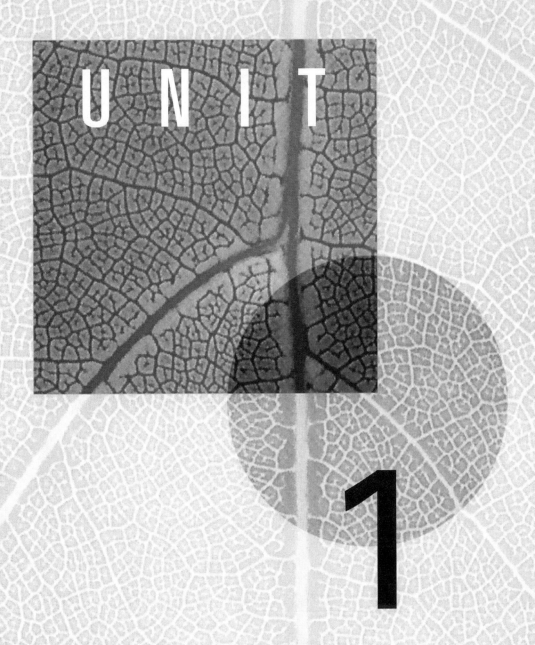

UNIT

1

Planning

Test Objectives: Planning

- Given a scenario, identify valid network configurations.

Exam objectives are subject to change at any time without prior notice and at Microsoft's sole discretion. Please visit Microsoft's Training & Certification Web site (www.microsoft.com/Train_Cert) for the most current exam objectives listing.

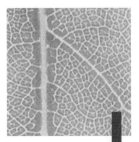

I dentifying a valid network configuration is largely a matter of knowing the rules. Read on to learn how to identify network classes and valid and reserved IP addresses and how subdividing your network affects the number of IP addresses available to you.

Identifying Valid Network Configurations

A TCP/IP network can be broken down as follows:

- An *internet* is a TCP/IP network divided into two or more connected parts, called *subnets*.

- A *subnet* is a subsection of an internet, defined for administrative purposes or to cut down on broadcast traffic, as all messages on a network are "heard" by all hosts whether the message is for that host or not. Messages sent from one host to another within the same subnet do not need to be routed, but messages sent between hosts in different subnets must be routed. Subnets are connected by *routers*, or *default gateways*.

- A *host* is any server or workstation on an IP network.

Figure 1.1 shows the relationship between internets, subnets, and hosts.

FIGURE 1.1

Internets, subnets, and hosts

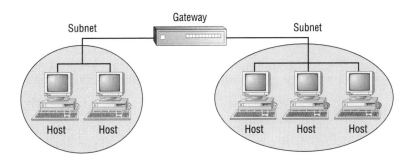

IP Addressing

An *IP address* is a 32-bit value assigned to a workstation, a server, or any other addressable node on a TCP/IP network. Not all IP addresses are available for hosts; some are reserved for other uses (see "Reserved Addresses" below).

Generally, there's a ratio of one IP address to one node. If a host has more than one network card, however, it will have two IP addresses. Network cards may also have more than one address.

An IP address has a hierarchical structure—part of it designates the *network address*, and part, the *host address*.

Dotted Quad Format

For convenience in nomenclature, each IP address is normally referred to in its *dotted quad format*, which divides the binary address into 4 parts and converts each part to decimal. Thus, every section of an IP address will be a value in the range 0 to 255, because 2 to the 8th power is 256 and IP addresses begin numbering at zero.

Class A, B, and C Networks

If you're creating an intranet that will never be connected to *the* Internet, you don't have to worry much about IP addressing—just assign your own. However, if you ever plan to talk to the rest of the world, you'll have to ask the NIC (Network Information Center) to assign you a block of IP addresses. It will do so based on your company's size:

- The very biggest companies get *Class A* addresses, for which the NIC determines only the first 8 bits of the address; the company can internally assign the other 24.

- Second-tier networks get *Class B* addresses, for which the NIC assigns the first 16 bits.

- Third-tier networks get *Class C* addresses, for which the NIC assigns the first 24 bits.

Table 1.1 defines each of the network classes.

T A B L E 1.1:   Network classes compared

	Format	Begins with Value	# of Hosts*	Example
Class A	net.host.host.host	0–126	Up to 16, 777, 214	122.40.76.3
Class B	net.net.host.host	128–191	Up to 65,535	180.75.28.92
Class C	net.net.net.host	192–223	Up to 256	201.68.114.2

* $(2^n)-2$ where n = number of bits in the host portion of the IP address

Values in the range 224 to239 (Class D) are reserved for multicast addresses, and values in the range 240 to 255 (Class E) are reserved for experimental ones. The address 127.0.0.1 is reserved as a loopback address, intended to let you be sure that your network card is functioning properly. A message sent to this IP address will return to you unless something is wrong with the network.

Classless Internet Domain Routing

No more Class A or Class B addresses are available or have been for a long time—even Microsoft has a Class B network. Because a large number of networks are now part of the Internet, even Class C addressing didn't offer enough flexibility, so the NIC has begun to assign addresses in which more than the first three quads are preassigned. For example, the NIC might assign your company an address that specifies the first 28 bits of the address, leaving you only 16 IP addresses—not a lot, but enough for many small companies. This newer method of assigning addresses is called *Classless Internet Domain Routing (CIDR)*. A CIDR network is described as a "slash-*n*" network, where *n* is the number of preassigned bits. The network in the example would be a "slash-28" network.

Reserved Addresses

You can't use all numbers in the block of IP addresses that you're assigned:

- Whatever your assigned address, the address that ends in all binary zeros (like 201.68.11.0) is the network number, the address that refers to the range of addresses in a subnet. You cannot assign this address to a host.

- The address that ends in all binary ones (like 201.88.11.255) is the TCP/IP broadcast address. A message sent to this address is broadcast to each machine on the subnet.

 If your network has a router, it will need its own IP address.

Subnet Masks

In a TCP/IP network, routers determine on which subnet an address is located by comparing the address to the *subnet mask*, a number that looks like an IP address. A predetermined set of bits must match for the IP address to be in the same subnet as the router—if it's not, the message sent to that address is passed along to the next subnet.

For example, if your Class C network had two subnets, you'd probably divide the addresses fairly evenly, up to decimal 128. Subnet masks are created by assigning 1s to network bits and 0s to host bits. Thus, your subnet mask might look like this for one subnet:

111111111 11111111 11111111 10000000

so the values within that subnet only vary within the last *seven* bits, and like this for another:

111111111 11111111 11111111 00000000

so that values within that subnet may vary for all eight bits.

The base subnet mask for a Class C network is always 255.255.255.0, meaning that the first three quads always match but the fourth can be any 8-bit number. Similarly, the base subnet mask for a Class A network would be 255.0.0.0, and for a Class B network, 255.255.0.0.

Thus, when the router on the first subnet hears a packet broadcast on the network, it checks the destination address of the packet against its subnet mask. If the IP address for the destination proves not to match the local subnet mask, the router forwards the packet.

In Figure 1.2, a router has two IP addresses—one on each subnet. When a packet is transmitted on Subnet A, the router "hears" it and examines the destination address, comparing it with the local subnet mask to detect whether the address is on the local subnet. If it is not, the packet is forwarded to the next subnet, where (if applicable) the router examines it again, determining whether the packet's subnet mask matches the one for the local router.

FIGURE 1.2

Using subnet masks to determine whether to route a packet

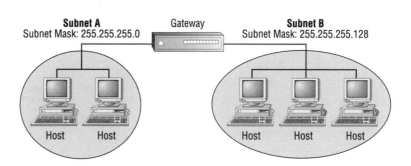

Subnet A — Subnet Mask: 255.255.255.0   Gateway   Subnet B — Subnet Mask: 255.255.255.128

Host   Host   Host   Host   Host

Each time you create another subnet, you lose two IP addresses to administrative overhead because of those reserved addresses mentioned earlier. Thus, more subnets mean fewer hosts.

Whether broadcasts can be routed depends on their type. Limited broadcasts (255.255.255.255) are sent only to the local subnet and not normally forwarded. Directed broadcasts (IP addresses with .255 in the final quad) are forwarded to the appropriate subnet.

1. You have 25 sites and expect to grow by 5 sites a year for the next 3 years. Each site will have 200 computers. If the network IP address is 152.60.0.0, what subnet mask will supply the minimum number of subnets and the maximum number of hosts?

_____

2. You are given a network address of 198.201.40.0 and a subnet mask of 255.255.255.224. What is the maximum number of hosts per subnet that you could create?

_____

3. You have received the address 198.201.40.0 from the NIC. What is the maximum number of hosts you can support without subnetting?

_____

4. You have received the address of 198.201.40.0 from the NIC. What is the maximum number of subnets that you could create?

_____

5. Given the following two IP addresses on the same network, provide a valid subnet mask. Use whole octets for subnetting. 130.40.50.60 and 130.40.50.70

_____

6. The NIC has assigned you a network ID of 204.30.77.0, and you want to subnet it for 14 subnets with 10 to 12 hosts per subnet. What subnet mask should you choose?

_____

7. How many host IP addresses per subnet are available for assignment on the network 129.76.35.0 with a subnet mask of 255.255.252.0?

_____

8. What subnet mask is required on a Class B network to provide 30 subnets?

_____

9. You are assigned a network address of 192.192.191.0 and want to begin assigning IP addresses to your hosts. What two addresses may not be assigned out of this address space?

_____

10. What is the maximum number of subnets available to the IP network 192.34.50.0?

_____

11. What is the limited broadcast address for IP network 130.25.0.0?

_____

12. What is the directed broadcast address for IP network 193.192.34.0?

_____

13. What class IP address provides many hosts but few networks?

_____

14. What class IP address provides many networks but few hosts?

_____

15. What is the address 224.0.0.0 in the routing table used for?

_____

16. You have installed an NT Server with two Ethernet adapters: One adapter serves a BNC network and is addressed as 140.50.2.3 with a subnet mask of 255.255.0.0; the other is 10BaseT and is addressed as 193.204.220.198 with a subnet mask of 255.255.255.0. You have a Unix host with an address of 140.50.2.4 and a Windows for Workgroups client with an address of 193.204.220.199. What should the default gateway be for the Windows for Workgroups client?

_____

17. A router has an Ethernet IP address of 190.4.4.1, a serial WAN link addressed as 190.3.3.1 to headquarters, a Token Ring interface addressed as 190.2.2.1 to the corporate mainframe, and a PPP connection to the Internet addressed as 190.1.1.1. What should an Ethernet user choose as the best default gateway for their TCP/IP configuration?

_____

18. A router has an Ethernet IP address of 190.4.4.1, a serial WAN link addressed as 190.3.3.1 to headquarters, a Token Ring interface addressed as 190.2.2.1 to the corporate mainframe, and a PPP connection to the Internet addressed as 190.1.1.1. What IP address should be entered for a Token Ring user as the best default gateway for their TCP/IP configuration?

_____

19. What is the minimum number of IP addresses a gateway may be assigned?

_____

20. You have installed an NT Server with two Ethernet adapters: One adapter serves a BNC network and is addressed as 140.50.2.3 with a subnet mask of 255.255.0.0; the other is 10BaseT and is addressed as 193.204.220.198 with a subnet mask of 255.255.255.0. You have a Unix host with an address of 140.50.2.4 and a Windows for Workgroups client with an address of 193.204.220.199. What should the default gateway be for the Unix client?

_____

SAMPLE TEST

1-1   You have a large LAN you want to segment with a 6-port router. Assuming a Class C address, what mask should you use?

    A. 255.255.255.0

    B. 255.255.255.224

    C. 255.255.255.248

    D. 255.255.255.192

    E. 255.255.224.0

1-2   Choose the best answer. Three hosts are on separate segments from one another connected by a single router with three interfaces.

    A. Each host will have a different subnet mask.

    B. Each host will have a different default gateway.

    C. Each host will have a different limited broadcast address.

    D. Each host will have the same default gateway.

    E. Each host will have a different loopback address.

1-3   Which of the following is not a valid host address on a Class C network? (Choose all that apply.)

    A. 200.48.17.1

    B. 190.64.90.2

    C. 198.200.87.0

    D. 240.78.99.15

UNIT

2

Installation and Configuration

Test Objectives: Installation and Configuration

- Given a scenario, select the appropriate services to install when using TCP/IP on a Microsoft Windows NT Server computer.

- On a Windows NT Server computer, configure Microsoft TCP/IP to support multiple network adapters.

- Configure scopes by using DHCP Manager.

- Install and configure a WINS server.
  - Import LMHOSTS files to WINS.
  - Run WINS on a multihomed computer.
  - Configure WINS replication.
  - Configure static mappings in the WINS database.

- Configure subnet masks.

- Configure a Windows NT Server computer to function as an IP router.
  - Install and configure the DHCP Relay Agent.

- Install and configure the Microsoft DNS Server service on a Windows NT Server computer.
  - Integrate DNS with other name servers.
  - Connect a DNS server to a DNS root server.
  - Configure DNS server roles.

- Configure HOSTS and LMHOSTS files.

- Configure a Windows NT Server computer to support TCP/IP printing.

- Configure SNMP.

Exam objectives are subject to change at any time without prior notice and at Microsoft's sole discretion. Please visit Microsoft's Training and Certification Web site (www.microsoft.com/Train_Cert/) for the most current listing of exam objectives.

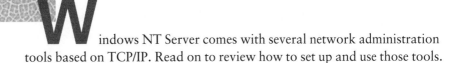indows NT Server comes with several network administration tools based on TCP/IP. Read on to review how to set up and use those tools.

Selecting a Service

Windows NT comes with three TCP/IP-based name resolution services:

- The Windows Internet Name Service (WINS)
- The Domain Name System (DNS)
- The Dynamic Host Configuration Protocol (DHCP)

Each service is designed for a specific use and works with the others (see Table 2.1).

	Service	Function
T A B L E 2.1 Windows NT TCP/IP-based administration tools	WINS	Provides local name resolution between IP addresses and NetBIOS names.
	DNS	Cooperates with the Internet DNS and WINS to resolve names with IP addresses for people connecting remotely.
	DHCP	Leases IP addresses to hosts for a time to avoid the need for static mapping of addresses to computers. With DHCP, only a few hosts (such as the name resolution servers and the default gateways) must have fixed IP addresses.

Thus, you'd use WINS for NetBIOS resolution, DNS for host resolution (technically, your DNS server does not have to be the one included with Windows NT Server; any DNS service will do), and DHCP to simplify the task of assigning IP addresses on your network.

Before the introduction of DHCP, to assign IP addresses on the network you had to maintain a text-based list of addresses on each computer and update those lists any time an addressing change was made to the network.

Configuring TCP/IP for Use in Multiple-Adapter Systems

You can set up Windows NT Server machines as routers in a network, connecting two subnets. To act as a router, a machine needs two (or more) IP addresses, perhaps from having more than one network card installed or a dial-up RAS connection to the network. Such a machine is called a *multi-homed* computer.

A multihomed computer is any computer with more than one IP address. Thus, a multihomed computer can have more than one network adapter or more than one IP address assigned to its adapter (or both). You can assign five IP addresses to a single adapter via the Network applet in Control Panel, and you can assign more via the Registry.

If you want the two adapters to communicate so that they can route packets from one network to another, you must set up IP forwarding between them. To do so, follow these steps:

1. Open the Network applet in Control Panel and select the Protocols tab.

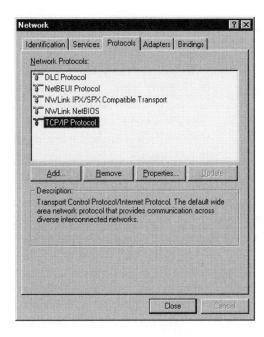

2. Click Properties to open the Microsoft TCP/IP Properties dialog box.

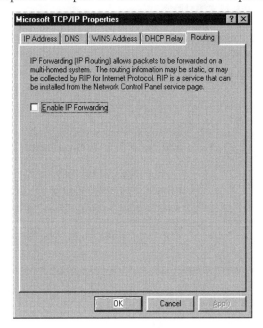

3. Select the Routing tab, check Enable IP Forwarding, and click OK.

Configuring Scopes with DHCP Manager

DHCP, the Dynamic Host Configuration Protcol, is derived from BOOT/P (not supported by Windows NT) and is a method of dynamically assigning IP addresses to hosts on the network for a predetermined period called a *lease*. When a host joins the network, it broadcasts a Dhcprequest packet to the network, requesting an IP address. If the host still has time left on a preexisting lease, it's reassigned the same IP address it had before. Otherwise, it's assigned a new address.

Statically defined IP addresses override DHCP assignments, so you cannot use DHCP to correct problems of faulty IP address configuration.

When you install DHCP Server on your computer via the Services tab in the Network applet, the DHCP Manager is automatically added to the Administrative Tools (Common) program group.

Creating a Scope

A DHCP *scope* consists of the following:

- A unique pool of IP addresses on a given subnet
- A valid subnet mask for that pool
- A defined set of IP addresses within the pool that are not available for lease, such as network addresses, default gateway addresses, or the addresses of name resolution servers.
- A lease time (three days is the default, but it can be configured to a longer or shorter time) that defines how long an address can be assigned to a given client before the address can be reassigned
- A scope name, defined by the DHCP administrator

Any Windows NT network on which IP addresses are to be dynamically assigned must have a DHCP server.

Start the DHCP Manager and choose Scope ➤ Create (see Figure 2.1).

FIGURE 2.1

Configuring scopes on
the local machine

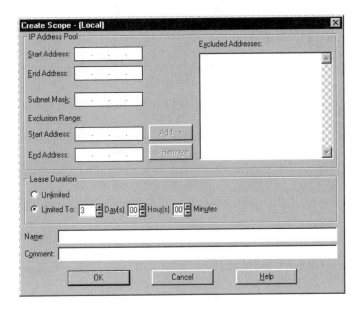

Define the range of addresses to be used on the subnet with the Start Address
and End Address blanks. Define a subnet mask, or use the one provided
that's based on the range of addresses you supplied. To exclude specific
addresses within that range, enter them in the Exclusion Range section and
click the Add button to add them to the list of excluded addresses.

You can specify more than one range to exclude.

The excluded addresses should include the following:

- Other DHCP servers

- Name resolution servers such as DNS and WINS servers

- RAS clients if you're not using DHCP to supply addresses for them

- Diskless workstations

Be sure to either exclude the address of the local DHCP Server or be sure that
it's not part of the pool.

> To exclude a single IP address, enter it in the Start Address box of the Exclusion Range section and leave the End Address box empty.

In the Lease Duration section, define the lease time for IP addresses, either sticking with the default or defining a range.

The proper lease time depends on the situation. If the number of IP addresses available is close to the number of hosts that need addresses or if hosts tend to leave and rejoin the network fairly frequently, a shorter lease time is in order. When a computer leaves the network and rejoins, it does not automatically lose its lease, but broadcasts a request for an IP address and finishes its lease.

Any computer with a Windows operating system can be a DHCP client, but only Windows NT Server 4 machines can be DHCP servers.

Assigning DHCP Options

When you finish creating a scope, DHCP Manager asks whether you want to activate it; you must activate at least one scope. Before activating it, define the DHCP options for the scope (or all scopes) using the DHCP Manager's Options menu. These options define how a DHCP client is configured:

Scope   Options apply only to the selected scope.

Global   Options apply to all scopes, but will be overridden by any scope-specific options.

Defaults   Options become the default for all scopes, but can be amended on a scope-by-scope basis.

Client   If a client has a static IP address, you can configure options for it specifically. These options will override any global or scope settings.

DHCP Server supports about 60 options, but not all are supported by all clients. The DHCP options that Windows NT–based and Windows-based clients support, and that can be set in the DHCP Options dialog box, are described in Table 2.2.

	Option	Description
TABLE 2.2 Windows-compatible DHCP options	3 Router	Supplies IP addresses for routers on the subnet. This option is equivalent to the default gateway setting.
	6 DNS Servers	Supplies IP addresses for DNS servers on the subnet.
	15 Domain Name	Defines the DNS domain name the client should use for host name resolution.
	44 WINS/NBNS Servers	Supplies a list of IP addresses for WINS or NetBIOS Name Servers.
	46 WINS/NBT Node Type	Allows NBT (NetBIOS over TCP/IP) configurable clients to be configured as described in RFC 1001 and 1002 (b-node, p-node, m-node, and h-node). Must be used in combination with 44.

Installing and Configuring WINS

T he Windows Internet Naming System (WINS) is a means of maintaining a dynamic database of IP addresses and the NetBIOS names to which they resolve. When they join the network, clients connect to the WINS server directly, rather than broadcasting their name and IP address information.

Like DNS and DHCP, WINS is not automatically installed during Windows NT Server Setup. To install it, activate the Network applet in the Control Panel and move to the Services tab (see Figure 2.2).

FIGURE 2.2

Preparing to install WINS

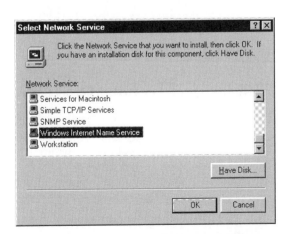

Click the Add button and choose Windows Internet Name Service in the list of available services to install. Supply the path to the installation files (such as D:\i386 if installing from the Windows NT Server CD-ROM in drive D) and let it go. When the files are copied, click Close, and then restart the machine as prompted.

The WINS service should begin when you restart, and the WINS Manager (see Figure 2.3) will be in the Administrative Tools (Common) program group.

FIGURE 2.3

The WINS Manager

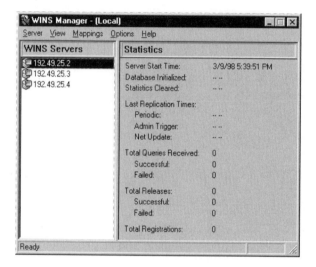

When a WINS client joins the network, it registers its name and IP address with the WINS server. When a host leaves the network, its name is not released. The client can rejoin the network without problems, however, just by registering its name as long as no other WINS clients have registered the same name in its absence. By default, WINS clients re-register their names every 96 hours even if still on the network This is called the *registration interval.*

Importing LMHOSTS Files to WINS

LMHOSTS files are static mappings of IP addresses to NetBIOS names. Once you've installed WINS, you can import an LMHOSTS file so that all computers with access to the WINS server can consult that database of static IP-NetBIOS mappings. This list needs updating only when changes occur.

To import an LMHOSTS file, run the WINS Manager and choose Static Mappings from the Mappings menu (see Figure 2.4). Click on the Import Mappings file, and browse for the file to import.

FIGURE 2.4

Importing an LMHOSTS file

 The primary LMHOSTS file on each computer is always in the \System32\Drivers\Etc folder of the Windows NT Server installation.

Running WINS on a Multihomed Computer

When a WINS client is multihomed (has two or more network cards, each with its own IP address), WINS performs some load balancing, distributing name resolutions equally between the two cards. You simply supply two different names for the WINS client at the same IP address.

Configuring WINS Replication

Microsoft recommends installing more than one WINS server on a network, replicating data between them, for two reasons:

- Better load balancing
- Better data redundancy for disaster recovery

If you have two or more WINS servers on the network, each is configured as a *pull partner* or a *push partner* of at least one other WINS server:

- Pull partners request database updates from their push partners, asking for records with a higher version number than those they already have. These updates can occur periodically (the WINS administrator sets the exact time interval), or the WINS administrator can initiate and update by sending a Replicate Now message in the WINS Manager.

- Push partners send messages to their pull partners about database changes. Prompted by this notification, the pull partners request the updates, at which point the push partners send a copy of the new/revised entries to their pull partners. Push partners send messages when a specified number of WINS entries are changed (the WINS administrator sets the exact number) or when the WINS administrator manually sends a replication message from WINS Manager.

Microsoft recommends that WINS servers be push partners and pull partners for each other. The primary and backup WINS servers *must* be push and pull partners for each other so as to make the primary WINS database backups consistent.

To set up WINS replication, choose Replication Partners from the Server menu in WINS Manager. Be sure that at least two WINS servers exist on the network.

If you haven't yet told WINS Manager about another WINS server on the network, you can do so from the Replication Partners dialog box by clicking the Add button and supplying the correct IP address.

WINS servers after the first one are automatically made push and pull partners to the primary WINS server. To make them only one or the other, check or uncheck the appropriate box in the Replication Partners dialog box (see Figure 2.4). To configure the update interval (for pull partners) or the update count (for push partners), click on the Configure button in the same area, and supply the proper number.

Configuring Static Mappings

Static mappings are permanent lists of name-to-IP address mappings that remain constant even if most of the network is using DHCP servers to lease IP addresses. The static mappings on your network may vary, but may include the DNS server, the gateway, and the DHCP server. You can import static mappings from an LMHOSTS file or enter them manually.

To create static mappings, choose Static Mappings from the Mappings menu. Click on the Add button in the Static Mappings dialog box, and in the Add Static Mappings dialog box that appears (see Figure 2.5), fill in the name and IP address of the entry.

FIGURE 2.5

Adding a new static mapping to the database

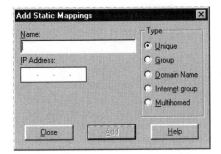

In the Type section, you have the following options:

Unique indicates that only one address is assigned to this name.

Group specifies a normal group in which individual IP addresses are not stored but name packets are broadcast to the group.

Domain Name is used by browsers to elect a master browser. It's the group of the 24 Windows NT primary or backup domain controllers in the domain. Other names not in the static mapping are added as they join the domain, as long as fewer than 25 names are already in the domain name group. If 25 names already exist, any names recorded at another WINS server will be deleted from the group, or the oldest member will be replaced by the newest one.

Internet Group is a user-defined group that stores a maximum of 25 IP addresses (such as a group of e-mail addresses linked under a single name).

In Windows NT 3.51, the Domain Name Type did not exist, but was known as the Internet Group type.

Multihomed is similar to a unique name except that it may refer to as many as 25 IP addresses all in use by a single multihomed computer.

Configuring Subnet Masks

Many TCP/IP networks are divided into two or more segments with slightly different network addresses—that is, they're subnetted. When a message is sent on a subnetted network, the routers on the network must decide whether the message's recipient is local and can hear the message if broadcast or is located on another segment and must be forwarded. Thus, you need *subnet masks* to help hosts identify which part of the address is individual to a network and which is the host address.

Even if your network is not subnetted, you'll still need to supply a default subnet mask: 255.0.0.0 (Class A networks), 255.255.0.0 (Class B networks), or 255.255.255.0 (Class C networks).

In each network class, a certain number of bits already define the network. For example, in Class A networks, 8 bits define the network, and the other 24 define host addresses. When subnet masks are introduced, additional bits are used to define network location. The number of additional bits used to define network location signifies the number of subnets.

For example, say you have a Class C network. The NIC defines the first 24 bits of all your network's IP addresses, leaving you 8 to define hosts. If you have subnets, you'll use some of those "host bits" to define networks within your main network. The number of "host bits" you use to define subnets determines the number of subnets you get. Your base Class C network address might look like this:

11000000 00110000 01001011 00000000

To define a subnet, you'd need to turn some of those zeros in the fourth quad (those being the only ones over which you have any discretion) to 1s, like this:

11000000 00110000 01001011 10000000

Each time you subnet, you lose some IP addresses to administrative overhead, as each subnet requires two host addresses:

- The network address

- The broadcast address

Table 2.3 shows how many subnets you'll get for a variety of masks on a Class C network and how many IP addresses will be on each subnet, both counting before the administrative overhead of two addresses per division.

T A B L E 2.3: Relating subnet masks to the number of subnets and hosts on a Class C network

Number of Subnets	IP Addresses Per Subnet	Bits Used	Subnet Masks
2	127	1	255.255.255.128
4	63	2	255.255.255.192
8	31	3	255.255.255.224
16	15	4	255.255.255.240
32	7	5	255.255.255.248
64	3	6	255.255.255.252
128	2	7	255.255.255.254

You can't practically divide a Class C network into more than perhaps 16 subnets, and you can't do it at all for more than 32 because you won't have any IP addresses to give to hosts after accounting for the network address, the broadcast address, and the address of the default gateway.

To determine the number of IP addresses per subnet at each number of subnets, count the zero bits left after the subnet mask has been applied, and make them binary 1s, converting that number to decimal.

Configuring a Windows NT Server IP Router

A Windows NT IP router connects two or more physical TCP/IP networks, providing routing services so that packets can be delivered between the two networks and so that packets not intended for the local subnet can be delivered. To make a Windows NT Server machine an IP router, in the TCP/IP Properties dialog box, select the Routing tab and then check the Enable IP Forwarding box.

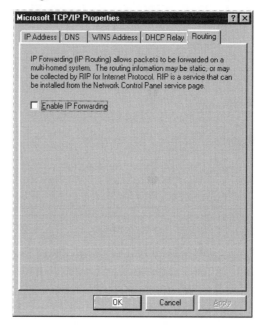

Route Tables

If a router connects more than two subnets, it doesn't just blindly forward all packets with destination addresses to all subnets—if it did, it would create more traffic problems than it would solve. Instead, it maintains *route tables* to help it decide which is the most likely path to the destination subnet and then forwards the packet accordingly. Doing so minimizes the number of times a packet must be forwarded—reduces the number of hops required—thus speeding up packet delivery and reducing network traffic. Route tables can be maintained either dynamically or statically.

Dynamic maintenance of route tables increases network traffic because routers must broadcast their routing information, but on changing networks simplifies the task of keeping routing tables up-to-date.

Dynamic Route Tables

For TCP/IP dynamic routing, these routing tables are built with the help of the Routing Information Protocol (RIP), a service that allows a Windows NT router to broadcast its routes and collect those of other routers, thus maintaining dynamic routing tables. To install this service, open the Network applet and select the Services tab. Once it's installed, it will automatically enable IP forwarding.

If RIP is installed on a machine with only a single IP address, the machine goes into *silent mode*, collecting routing information but not broadcasting any of its own.

RIP will collect routing information, updating the best paths to use as routers are added to or deleted from the network.

Static Route Tables

If your network doesn't change much, you can decrease network traffic by configuring static route tables with the ROUTE command, which has the following syntax:

```
route [-f] [-p] [command [destination] [MASK netmask]
[gateway] [METRIC metric]]
```

Table 2.4 explains the switches in this command.

TABLE 2.4	Switch	What It Does/Is
The switches in the ROUTE command	-f	Clears the routing table of all current entries. If you use the -f switch, it takes effect before any commands also specified.
	-p	Enables persistent routes so that route paths are maintained from reboot to reboot.
	command	Is one of the following commands: print to print a route; add to add a route; delete to delete a (single) route; change to modify an existing route.
	destination	The host or network to which you want to route.
	MASK	Specifies that the next parameter entered is the subnet mask to be associated with the route entry (the netmask value).
	netmask	The subnet mask for the destination. If no value is supplied, the subnet mask is assumed to be 255.255.255.255.
	gateway	The gateway to the specified destination.
	METRIC	Specifies that the next parameter entered is the metric.
	metric	Specifies the distance (in hops) to the destination. If no value is supplied, the metric is assumed to be 1, meaning that it's on the local subnet.

For example, this command:

```
route add 192.48.41.0 mask 255.255.255.0 192.48.40.1 metric 3
```

means that, to get to network 192.48.41.0 with subnet mask 255.255.255.0, the computer should use gateway 192.48.40.1, three hops away.

The next router will need a static entry to direct it to subnets accessible from the first router. The more routers in the network, the more complicated the route tables.

You must uninstall RIP to use static route tables.

Installing the DHCP Relay Agent

When any Microsoft client joins a TCP/IP network, it broadcasts an ARP packet in order to verify that the IP address that it's using is unique and, if using DHCP, issues a request for an IP address from the DHCP server. These addressing announcements are not normally forwarded to other subnets. You'll need the DHCP Relay Agent to make a Windows NT Server machine capable of routing DHCP messages from one subnet to another, so that a client on one subnet can request an IP lease from a DHCP server on another subnet. This is necessary unless you want to maintain one DHCP server per subnet.

To install the DHCP Relay Agent, activate the Network applet in the Control Panel and select the Services tab. Click on the Add button, and choose DHCP Relay Agent from the list of services to install. Indicate the path for the program files, supply an address for a DHCP server when prompted, and then close the Network applet when you're done. Restart the machine as prompted. The DHCP Relay Agent will start automatically when Windows NT starts again.

Configuring the DHCP Relay Agent

The settings for the DHCP Relay Agent are set in the Properties sheet for TCP/IP, in the Network applet in the Control Panel. Select the DHCP Relay tab (see Figure 2.6).

Enter the IP address of the DHCP server, and (if necessary) edit the entries for the seconds threshold and maximum hops. By default, the maximum hop value is 4, but RIP (the protocol used to relay the information) can support as many as 15 hops.

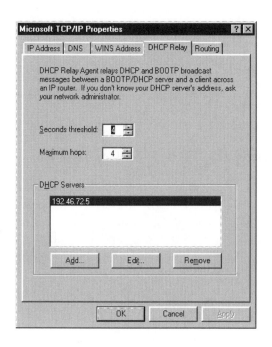

Installing and Configuring DNS

DNS (Domain Name System) is the Windows NT service that reconciles Internet addresses with IP addresses. It's much like WINS in function, except that it resolves host names, instead of NetBIOS names.

Installing DNS

To install DNS, select the Services tab of the Network applet in Control Panel, and click Add. Choose Microsoft DNS Server from the list, supply the path to the installation files, and reboot when prompted.

When you reboot, the DNS Manager (see Figure 2.7) will be in the Administrative Tools (Common) program group.

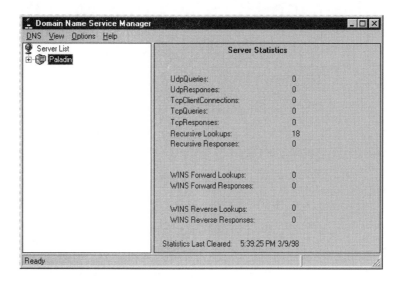

Configuring DNS

When you first open the DNS Manager, it contains no information for the
local network and is a caching-only name server for the Internet, with information about DNS root servers (the .com, .mil, .org, and so forth servers
that organize packets by the domain of their destination).

First, you need to add all DNS servers to the list. To do so, choose New
Server from the DNS menu and fill in the names or IP addresses of the servers
(including the local computer).

Next, define the zones on each server. The core administrative unit for
DNS maintenance is called a *zone*. You can have a root zone as well as
smaller zones that encompass a limited part of the local network. For best
data security, you can set up a domain on two DNS servers: a primary one
on one server and a secondary one that is a copy of the primary on another.
This is called *zone transfer*.

Configuring HOSTS and LMHOSTS Files

HOSTS and LMHOSTS files are ASCII text files used for name resolution. HOSTS files are used like DNS for resolution between IP addresses and fully qualified domain names; LMHOSTS files are used like WINS for resolving NetBIOS names to IP addresses.

Configuring HOSTS Files

The format for a HOSTS file is simple. Each host's IP address and its name go on one line, beginning with the IP address, like this:

```
200.32.58.12 ams.isinglass.com
200.32.58.25 serpent.isinglass.com
```

To make comments in the file, preface the statement to be commented with a hash mark (#). If you put the hash mark at the beginning of a line, the entire line is commented.

The only catch to using HOSTS files for name resolution is that one copy of HOSTS must reside on each computer so that it can do name resolution. Whenever you change IP address name mappings, you must make that change on every PC.

Table 2.5 shows how HOSTS files are stored for each operating system, including the sample HOSTS file.

T A B L E 2.5 Storing HOSTS files	**Operating System**	**Where Stored**
	Windows NT	In the \System32\Drivers\Etc folder of the Windows NT directory
	Windows for Workgroups	In the Windows directory
	Windows 95	In the Windows directory
	Others (such as DOS or OS/2)	In the same directory as the networking software

HOSTS files have their place in small networks not using DNS for name resolution or as a backup in case the DNS server goes down. You can't, of course, use them for any IP addresses within a DHCP scope, as those values will not be fixed.

Configuring LMHOSTS Files

The process of creating an LMHOSTS file is similar to that of creating a HOSTS file, but more options are available to you. LMHOSTS files can replace HOSTS files and fill more functions (similar to those of WINS).

Table 2.6 list the LMHOSTS keywords and shows how you can use them to improve name resolution performance and organize IP addresses.

T A B L E 2.6:   LMHOSTS keywords

Keyword	Purpose	Syntax
#INCLUDE	Permits marked addresses in an LMHOSTS file to be added to a global file that may supplement local LMHOSTS files. This keyword must be used in combination with #PRE to preload the names into the cache, and it can be used with #BEGIN ALTERNATE and #END ALTERNATE to define a list of servers maintaining the same LMHOSTS file, rather than just a single server.	#INCLUDE IPAddress PCName
#BEGIN ALTERNATE, #END ALTERNATE	Define the beginning and end of the list of servers maintaining the same LMHOSTS file.	#BEGIN ALTERNATE #INCLUDE IPAddress PCName #INCLUDE IPAddress PCName #END ALTERNATE
#PRE	Loads that entry (and as many as 100 entries) into the name cache to achieve faster resolution. Without this keyword, entries are only parsed after WINS queries and broadcasts fail to resolve the name. This keyword must be used with all entries marked with the #INCLUDE keyword, and Microsoft recommends that it be used with all entries marked with the #DOM keyword.	IPAddress Name #PRE

T A B L E 2.6: LMHOSTS keywords *(continued)*

Keyword	Purpose	Syntax
#DOM	Indicates that the computer is a domain controller and adds entries to a domain name cache that speeds up the processing of requests sent to domain controllers.	IPAddress PCName #DOM:DomainName
#SG	Specifies that an entry is a member of a user-defined special group of as many as 25 members. These groups may be defined for easier browsing or for broadcasting to members of that group.	IPAddress PCName #SG:GroupName
#MH	Specifies that the entry is for a multi-homed computer (one with more than one IP address). One name can correspond to as many as 25 IP addresses.	

A sample LMHOSTS file is in the System32\Drivers\Etc folder of your Windows NT installation. The LMHOSTS file must be stored in this folder.

Setting Up TCP/IP Printing

Using the Line Printer Daemon (LPD), Windows NT Server machines can receive print jobs from clients running the Line Printer (LPR) protocol, whether those clients are running Unix or another operating system (Windows NT also supports LPR, for example). The TCP/IP Print Service, based on LPD, permits clients to print to printers attached to Unix computers, even if the clients cannot normally communicate with Unix systems.

Only the computer providing TCP/IP printing services must have TCP/IP installed; the clients sending need to have only a common protocol with the printer server, and the job is passed on from there.

In version 4, Windows NT's LPR protocol includes the following features:

- It supports multiple data files per control file.

- When used in "print through" mode, the host name is passed through the printing subsystem to identify print jobs by sender.

- More ports are available than with Windows NT 3.51, meaning that print jobs are less likely to be held up due to a shortage of ports.

Installing TCP/IP Printing

To install support for TCP/IP printing, turn to the Services tab of the Network applet in the Control Panel and choose to add a service. Choose Microsoft TCP/IP printing from the list of services and indicate the file source. When you restart the system, the service will be installed but not started, as it is set by default for manual startup.

To make TCP/IP Printing start each time you start Windows NT, activate the Services applet, highlight TCP/IP Printing in the list of installed services, and then click on the Startup button to make it begin automatically.

Adding TCP/IP Printers

Once the TCP/IP Print Service is installed, you can add TCP/IP printers with the Add Printer Wizard as you would add any other printer. The only additional information you need to supply is the IP address, the domain name of the printer, or the host to which it's connected. The LPR software needs this information to find the printer.

Don't supply the share name of the printer, but the name by which it's locally known.

Configuring SNMP

You can use the Simple Network Management Protocol (SNMP) for network software-based management, including:

- Remotely monitoring and configuring WINS servers

- Monitoring DHCP servers

- Monitoring TCP/IP-related performance counters with the Performance Monitor

- Using the SNMP-based utilities in the Windows NT Resource Kit

Support for SNMP is included with Windows NT in the form of the SNMP Service which can be installed from the Services tab of the Network applet in the Control Panel.

When you've copied the files to the server, you'll be prompted to configure the SNMP service (see Figure 2.8).

FIGURE 2.8

Configuring the SNMP Service

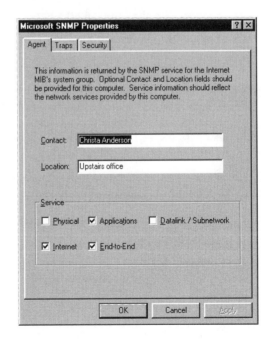

Using this Properties sheet, you'll define the following:

- The name of the person to be contacted when alerts occur (the Contact)

- The location of the computer on which the service is loaded

- The type of services for which SNMP will be used

- Destination for trap notices

- Which hosts the SNMP server should receive packets from (by default, any host)

Selecting a Service

1. Windows NT _____ server provides dynamic IP address assignment to its clients.

2. Windows NT Server _____ application provides NetBIOS name resolution to its clients.

3. You're making your HTTP server accessible to users via the Internet. What service(s) will you install to provide host name resolution?

_____

4. What kinds of names are resolved with the Windows Internet Name Service?

_____

5. What setting do you need to apply to make WINS resolve fully qualified domain names, without using another service?

_____

Configuring TCP/IP for Use in Multiple-Adapter Systems

6. A computer with more than one IP address is called a(n) _____ computer.

STUDY QUESTIONS

7.   True or False: A computer must be multihomed to communicate with a computer not on its subnet.

8.   Via the Network applet, you can assign a maximum of _____ IP addresses to a single adapter.

Configuring Scopes with DHCP Manager

9.   Give two situations in which it is recommended to create DHCP scopes with relatively short lease durations.

_____

_____

10.   True or False: The network administrator can use a DHCP scope-specific option to override an incorrectly specified TCP/IP configuration parameter on a client system.

11.   What IP address does a DHCP client use for the DHCP server when requesting an IP during its initialization? Specify the destination IP address in the client's request packet.

_____

12.   What mechanism in DHCP is used between DHCP servers to coordinate IP address assignments in the event of overlapping scope ranges and to ensure that no duplicate IP addresses are assigned?

_____

13. Under what circumstances is it recommended that the DHCP lease duration be increased?

_____

_____

14. True or False: When configuring multiple DHCP servers, it is best to have them all share the same IP address space so that they can back up one another.

15. What is required to be used as a Unique Identifier when adding a Reserved Client for DHCP configuration?

_____

16. True or False: By default, TCP/IP will use DHCP configuration on all adapters in a Windows NT system if Enable Automatic DHCP Configuration is checked.

17. What should be done to a DHCP scope after it has been created, but prior to its activation?

_____

18. What two items must be entered for a TCP/IP Client Installation if DHCP Automatic Configuration is not used?

_____

19. True or False: Windows NT systems can be configured to support BOOTP.

20.   True or False: When a DHCP client is shut down, it sends a message to the DHCP server to release its IP address lease.

21.   How should the WINS server's static IP address be entered into a DHCP server's scope?

_____

_____

22.   True or False: Windows NT now supports BOOTP.

23.   Dynamic Host Configuration Protocol is an extension of the _____ protocol.

24.   True or False: A WINS server can be installed with Automatic DHCP Configuration as long as the default gateway is correctly specified.

Installing and Configuring WINS

25.   You are configuring WINS for 4 remote sites. Site #1 is Headquarters; Site # 2, Site #3, and Site #4 are remote offices. You configure each remote site to be a push and pull replication partner with Headquarters. How many replication partners does Site #3 have?

_____

26. You are configuring WINS for 4 remote sites. Site #1 is Headquarters; Site # 2, Site #3, and Site #4 are remote offices. You configure each remote site to be a push and pull replication partner with headquarters. How many replication partners does Site #1 have?

_____

27. True or False: When a WINS registered client drops off the network without releasing its address, it must wait until the expiration period elapses or for a network administrator to delete the mapping to rejoin the network.

28. How do you configure primary and secondary WINS servers to be consistent replication partners with one another?

_____

_____

29. Define the WINS configuration term _Renewal Interval_.

_____

_____

30. WINS reduces the number of _____ on the local network segment.

31. For the databases on the primary and backup WINS servers to remain consistent, they must be both _____ and _____ replication partners with each other.

32. What other DHCP option must be set when the 044 WINS/NBNS Servers option is set?

_____

33. True or False: WINS eliminates the need for an LMHOSTS file.

34. True or False: WINS facilitates both intra-domain and inter-domain browsing.

35. List two benefits that WINS provides.

_____

_____

36. True or False: When a WINS client is shut down, it sends a message to the WINS server to release its name.

37. True or False: WINS is considered a static database used for name resolution.

Configuring Subnet Masks

38. True or False: A Class B address with a subnet mask of 255.255.255.0 has more host IP addresses available for assignment per subnet than a Class C address with no subnetting.

39. True or False: A Class B address with a subnet mask of 255.255.255.240 allows for more hosts per subnet than a Class C address with the same subnet mask.

40. How many subnets are available to a Class A address with a mask of 255.255.0.0?

_____

41. True or False: A Class C IP address with a subnet mask of 255.255.255.224 has fewer host IP addresses per subnet than a Class B IP address with the same subnet mask.

42. The default subnet mask for 40.75.57.4 is _____.

43. Your organization has been assigned the Internet address of 140.20.0.0 by the NIC. What is the class and what is the default subnet mask for this address?

_____

44. The NIC has assigned you an IP address of 208.207.205.0. What is the class of this network and what is the default subnet mask?

_____

45. You have been given an IP address of 204.16.30.5 and a default subnet mask. What is the maximum number of hosts on this network?

_____

46. You are given an IP address of 204.16.30.0, and you require at least 3 subnets with at least 10 hosts per subnet. Which two subnet masks could you use?

_____

47. You have been assigned a network address of 204.16.30.0. You require 6 subnets with at least 20 hosts per subnet. Specify the subnet mask you use to define the final subnet.

_____

48. You are given a network address of 145.45.0.0 and require 6 subnets. What subnet mask do you use to define the final subnet?

_____

49. The default subnet mask for 190.191.193.4 is _____.

50. Given that the first two bits of an IP address are 10 (binary), what is the default subnet mask (decimal)?

_____

51. The default subnet mask for 126.1.2.1 is _____.

52. What is the direct broadcast address for an IP network address of 140.50.30.10 with a subnet mask of 255.255.255.0?

_____

53. Given an IP address of 128.192.254.1, identify both the class and default subnet mask.

_____

54. You want to subnet the network 10.0.0.0 using only whole octets for subnetting. Given the IP addresses 10.20.30.40 and 10.20.40.30 on the same subnet, provide a valid subnet mask.

_____

55. How many hosts can you assign per subnet given an IP network address of 193.45.34.0 and a subnet mask of 255.255.255.248?

_____

56. You have a router attached to 3 Ethernet segments. There are 25 clients on one segment, a server and 20 clients on the second segment, and 5 servers and 10 clients on the third segment. You are given the address 204.30.45.0. Give the subnet mask that will provide the maximum growth for hosts.

_____

57. You have a router attached to 4 Ethernet segments. There are 13 clients on one segment, a server and 12 clients on the second segment, 4 servers and 17 clients on the third segment, and 3 servers and 11 clients on the fourth segment. What is the total number of IP addresses required?

_____

Configuring a Windows NT Server IP Router

58. True or False: A DHCP server is needed on every subnet of very large networks

59. True or False: Non–WINS-enabled clients may communicate with remote servers providing the intermediate routers are configured for DHCP Relay Agent to forward name query broadcasts.

60. The maximum hop count for RIP is _____.

61. How do you disable RIP routing on a Windows NT computer?

_____

62. What must be enabled on a Windows NT Server used on a DHCP network when the DHCP server is remote from your subnet?

_____

Installing and Configuring DNS

63. How do caching-only DNS servers get their information?

_____

_____

64. What file contains the names of the Internet root domain servers?

_____

_____

65. True or False: The DNS domain suffix search order uses the domain suffix appended to the short host name to perform DNS host name resolution.

66. True or False: To complete the configuration of DNS use for host name resolution, you must add the DNS name server's IP address to the HOSTS file.

67. DNS database replication between DNS servers is called

_____ .

68. Where does a secondary DNS server get its zone data file from?

_____

69. What is the primary benefit of using caching-only DNS servers?

_____

70. True or False: A recursive DNS name query means that the DNS server replies to the client with the IP address requested or with the name of the DNS server that can satisfy the request.

71. True or False: DNS may be used to resolve NetBIOS names to IP addresses.

72. True or False: A Windows NT DNS server can submit a query to WINS for name resolution.

73. Why should you create reverse-lookup zones in DNS before creating the host records?

_____

74. Clients in DNS transactions are called _____.

75. True or False: DNS is considered a static database used for name resolution.

76. What item must be configured on a client in order to use DNS host resolution?

_____

77. True or False: Broadcasts can be used to find a DNS name server in the event the IP address is not found in the local host table.

78. True or False: When assigning the host name for DNS on Windows NT system, the DNS host name must match the NetBIOS computer name with the scope ID suffix appended to it.

Configuring HOSTS and LMHOSTS Files

79. True or False: The #DOM directive is used in the HOSTS file to identify domain controllers.

80. You are configuring an NT system to communicate with a remote NT domain across a router in a non-WINS environment. The remote NT IP address is 163.84.56.6. The server NetBIOS name is Server4 in the GIANT domain. What must the LMHOSTS file entry look like?

_____

81. Type the entry for the hostname SERVER1, an alias of NTSERVER, and an IP address of 130.10.4.5 in the HOSTS file with the comment *test system*.

_____

82. You have installed a Unix server on an NT domain with 15 Windows for Workgroups clients. The domain does not use DNS. You have entered a valid HOSTS file on the NT server and have successfully tested communications with PING between the NT server and the Unix server. The Windows for Workgroups clients can FTP to the Unix server if they use its IP address. What should you do to enable them to use the Unix hostname?

_____

_____

83. You want to include a centralized LMHOSTS shared in the PUBLIC directory on the NT system named Server4, with IP address 126.90.10.6. What two entries must be made in your local LMHOSTS file? (Do not use the ALTERNATE directive.)

_____

_____

84. Multiple LMHOSTS files from remote servers can be specified as a group to be included in the local LMHOSTS file if the #INCLUDE directives begin with the _____ and end with the _____ directives.

85. The _____ directive in an LMHOSTS file will load mappings from a centralized file.

86. What file is used in a non-WINS environment to map NetBIOS names to IP addresses?

_____

87. What file is used to update static mappings using the Import Mappings function in WINS Manager?

_____

88. What directive in an LMHOSTS file will load a centralized LMHOSTS file?

_____

89. What directive in an LMHOSTS file will pre-load a NetBIOS name and IP address in the client's cache?

_____

90. True or False: The HOSTS file can be used for NetBIOS name resolutions.

Setting Up TCP/IP Printing

91. What TCP/IP command is used to print to a host running the LPD service?

_____

92. A Windows NT Server machine with the TCP/IP Print Service running is using NetBEUI and TCP/IP as its transport protocols. What protocol must clients use if they want to connect to the TCP/IP printer?

_____

93. By default, TCP/IP Printing is set for _____ startup.

94. True or False: TCP/IP Printing under Windows NT 4 supports multiple control files per data file.

95. What information must you supply to LPR to permit it to print to a TCP/IP printer?

_____

96. For purposes of connecting with LPR, a printer should be known by its

_____ name.

Configuring SNMP

97. Where do you specify the user name of the person who should receive SNMP alerts?

_____

98. True or False: By default, SNMP can receive packets from any host.

SAMPLE TEST

2-1 Select all answers that match the WINS filter range for the IP address 15.151.0.0.

    A. 15.1*1.*.*

    B. 15.*.*.*

    C. 1*.1*.*.*

    D. 15.151.255.255

    E. 15*.15*.0.0

2-2 Choose a phrase to complete the following sentence. Use of WINS
_____ Microsoft clients.

    A. Increases the number of IP broadcasts generated by

    B. Decreases the number of IP broadcasts generated by

    C. Does not effect the number of IP broadcasts generated by

    D. Decreases the number of ARP requests generated by

    E. Increases the number of ARP requests generated by

2-3 How many scopes may be created within DHCP for a single subnet?

    A. 5

    B. 1

    C. An unlimited number, but you need to use the Registry editor

    D. 2

    E. 10

2-4   What domain is configured by option 15 in DHCP?

    A. Windows NT Domain

    B. DNS Domain

    C. NIS Domain

    D. Default Domain

    E. Eminent Domain

2-5   A previously configured DHCP client that later reboots will send a
_____ message to the DHCP server during its IP
configuration.

    A. Dhcpdiscover

    B. Dhcpoffer

    C. Dhcprequest

    D. Dhcpack

    E. Dhcpnak

2-6   DNS was originally designed to replace the _____ file.

    A. LMHOSTS

    B. NAMES

    C. DOMAINS

    D. HOSTS

    E. SERVICES

SAMPLE TEST

2-7 The root level of the DNS name space is managed by:

    A. InterNIC

    B. Berkeley

    C. Microsoft

    D. Department of Defense

    E. UCLA

2-8 The DNS PTR record for the IP address 154.94.37.25 is:

    A. 154.94.37.25.inaddr.arpa

    B. in-addr.arpA.154.94.37.25

    C. 25.37.94.154.in-add-arpA.

    D. 25.37.94.154.in-addr.arpa

    E. inaddr-arpA.255.255.255.255

2-9 What type of DNS query is made when the client requests the host name by giving the host's IP address?

    A. Name

    B. Recursive

    C. Iterative

    D. Reverse

    E. Forward

SAMPLE TEST

2-10   A DNS server designated to communicate to a network external to the corporation is called:

   A. A forwarder

   B. A DNS relay server

   C. A fully recursive server

   D. A firewall

   E. An iterative server

2-11   You have a Class B network with a subnet mask of 255.255.255.0. Your Windows NT Server has an address of 140.50.30.70. Provide a valid address for a Windows for Workgroups client.

   A. 140.50.31.70

   B. 140.50.30.71

   C. 140.55.45.2

   D. 140.50.255.0

   E. 140.50.03.1

2-12   What dynamic routing protocol does Windows NT 4 use to update its routing tables?

   A. OSPF

   B. MPR

   C. DRP

   D. RIP

   E. UDP

2-13   After starting DNS Manager, you can port data files from a non-Microsoft DNS server by:

    A. Stopping DNS Manager, copying the files, and restarting DNS Manager.

    B. Copying the files, editing the Registry, then stopping and restarting DNS Manager.

    C. Copying the files only. DNS will port the files automatically when restarted.

    D. Using the command `bindupd - [filename]`.

    E. Using NSLOOKUP /NEW.

2-14   Microsoft's implementation of NBNS under RFC 1001/1002 is called:

    A. DHCP

    B. WINS

    C. DNS

    D. MPR

    E. RIP

2-15   Which of the following can be used by Microsoft clients when resolving names to IP addresses?

    A. DNS

    B. LMHOSTS file

    C. RESOLVER file

    D. HOSTS file

    E. SERVICE file

2-16   Which of the following *must* be entered to configure a DHCP server?

    A. DNS address

    B. IP address

    C. Primary WINS server

    D. Scope ID

    E. Subnet mask

2-17   You have a Class C network with 6 subnets. The 175 laptop clients frequently roam between these subnets. You should configure:

    A. DHCP server on each subnet with default lease time.

    B. Central DHCP server with short lease time.

    C. You have too many clients for this network.

    D. DHCP and WINS server on each subnet with long lease time.

    E. Central DHCP and DNS server with long lease time.

2-18   Server A is a primary WINS server, and Server B is the secondary WINS server. Choose a replication strategy from the following list:

    A. A is push partner, B is pull partner.

    B. A is push and pull partner, B is pull partner.

    C. A and B are push and pull partners.

    D. A is pull partner, B is push partner.

    E. A and B are replication partners by default.

SAMPLE TEST

2-19   A WINS push partner updates its pull partner by:

   A. Sending the entire WINS database to it

   B. Notifying the pull partner that it has updates

   C. Sending changes only without notification

   D. Requesting its version number

   E. Merging updates with the database

2-20   Which DHCP option type should be changed to configure the default gateway for multiple networks?

   A. Global

   B. Scope

   C. Default

   D. Router

   E. Gateway

2-21   Which DHCP option type should be changed to configure a single WINS server for multiple networks?

   A. Global

   B. Scope

   C. Default

   D. Router

   E. Gateway

SAMPLE TEST

2-22   Which of the following is/are benefits of DHCP?

   A. No need for user TCP/IP configuration

   B. No need to register the host name

   C. No need to reconfigure stations that change subnets

   D. No need for administrator to perform IP subnet calculations

   E. No need for DNS

2-23   Which is the recommended configuration for dual DHCP servers?

   A. Each 50% different IP address scopes

   B. Each 100% same IP address scopes

   C. One with 75%, the other with remaining 25%

   D. Each with 100% different IP address scopes

   E. Each with alternating IP address scopes

2-24   From which of the following protocols is DHCP derived?

   A. ICMP

   B. UDP

   C. SNMP

   D. BOOTP

   E. TCP

SAMPLE TEST

2-25   Which of the following may be a DHCP server? Choose all that apply.

   A. Windows for Workgroup 3.11

   B. Windows NT Workstation 3.51

   C. Windows NT Server 4

   D. Windows 95

   E. Windows NT Workstation 4

2-26   What does RIP use for a transport protocol?

   A. ARP

   B. TCP

   C. UDP

   D. IP

   E. iCMP

2-27   Which of the following may be a DHCP client? Choose all that apply.

   A. Windows for Workgroup 3.11

   B. Windows NT Workstation 3.51

   C. Windows NT Server 4

   D. Windows 95

   E. Windows NT Workstation 4

2-28   Which of the following is a valid IP address on a network with a host IP of 10.20.30.40 with a subnet mask of 255.255.0.0?

   A. 8.20.40.41

   B. 9.20.40.42

C. 10.20.30.41

D. 11.20.30.42

E. 10.02.03.05

2-29 What print destination is used for TCP/IP Printing to a Unix-host printer?

A. Digital Network Port

B. Local Port

C. LPR Port

D. Other...

E. LPQ Port

2-30 Which of the following is not set in the SNMP Properties dialog box? Choose all that apply.

A. The contact name

B. The contact e-mail address

C. The types of services for which SNMP will be used

D. The computers from which SNMP is capable of receiving packets

2-31 Entries in the LMHOSTS file with the #PRE directive should be:

A. Placed at the beginning of the file for faster loading into the cache

B. Placed at the end of the file, since they will not be accessed after TCP initializes

C. Placed anywhere in the file, since they are comments only

D. Left out of the LMHOSTS file, since #PRE only applies to the HOSTS file

E. Placed at the end, except when used with the #DOM directive

SAMPLE TEST

2-32 A DNS zone transfer:

    A. Copies only the changes from the primary to the secondary

    B. Copies the entire database from the primary to the secondary

    C. Copies the updates entered in the `DNSUPD.LOG` file from the primary to the secondary

    D. Copies the DNS cache from the primary to the secondary

    E. Copies the DNS cache from the secondary to the cache-only server

UNIT

3

Connectivity

Test Objectives: Connectivity

- Given a scenario, identify which utility to use to connect to a TCP/IP-based Unix host.

- Configure a RAS server and Dial-Up Networking for use on a TCP/IP network.

- Configure and support browsing in a multiple-domain routed network.

Exam objectives are subject to change at any time without prior notice and at Microsoft's sole discretion. Please visit Microsoft's Training and Certification Web site (www.microsoft.com/Train_Cert/) for the most current listing of exam objectives.

One of the main perks of using TCP/IP as your network's transport protocol is the flexibility it gives you. Read on to review the fundamentals of making that flexibility work for you in connecting to Unix, supplying remote access services, and browsing across domains.

Connecting to a Unix Host

Windows NT comes with several utilities that you can use to connect a Windows NT machine to a Unix host (see Table 3.1). Which you use depends on what you're trying to do.

T A B L E 3.1:   Windows NT–Unix connection utilities and their application

Utility	Application	Security
finger	Displays information about a specified user connected to a host running the finger service.	None.
ftp	Transfers files to and from a computer running the ftp service.	Password protected. Public ftp servers commonly let you log on with your user name and "anonymous" for a password.
lpr	Prints a file to a host running the lpd service.	User authentication is provided by the Windows NT Server domain.
rcp	Copies files between a Windows NT computer and a Unix computer running the rsh service.	Current or specified user name must exist in the remote host's RHOSTS file.

T A B L E 3.1: Windows NT–Unix connection utilities and their application *(continued)*

Utility	Application	Security
rexec	Runs commands on remote hosts with the rexec service running.	Use is password-protected.
rsh	Runs commands on remote hosts with the rsh service running.	Current or specified user name must exist in the remote host's RHOSTS file.
telnet	Terminal emulation program used to access character-based Unix programs to be run remotely.	User must have an account on the Unix server running the telnet service.
tftp	Creates a connectionless link between a client and server for file transfer.	User authentication is provided by the Windows NT Server domain.

Unless all these connection utilities are used in combination with their server utilities, they won't work. The nature of their failure depends on the type of link. For example, connection-oriented protocols (those running atop TCP) will report a failure, whereas connectionless utilities (those running atop the User Datagram Protocol (UDP) will only stop responding.

 For any of these utilities to work, the host's name must be resolved either in a HOSTS file on your computer or with DNS.

The RHOSTS file

Unit 2 described the HOSTS file as a static list of host names resolved to IP addresses, used when a DNS server is not available. Although it may also be supplanted by a DNS server, the RHOSTS file is somewhat different—its function is to provide a list of users who have permission to run commands on the remote host. The format is similar to that used in HOSTS files: the local computer name, the local user name, and any comments about the user, with comments being prefaced by a hash mark. A sample entry might look like this:

```
serpent    christa    #this is a comment
```

When you run `rsh`, `rexec`, or `rcp` to connect to a host with a properly configured RHOSTS file, you should not have to provide a name and password to use the utilities.

finger

The purpose of the `finger` utility is to get information about a user or users logged on to a specified host. The information that the host returns depends on the host itself. The command syntax is as follows:

```
finger [1] [username] @hostname [IP address]
```

The `1` argument displays the results in long list format and is not supported on all hosts.

If you don't supply the `username`, you're given information for everyone currently logged on to that host. You do need to supply the host's name or, alternatively, its IP address.

ftp

The `ftp` (File Transfer Protocol) utility is used for transferring files between server and client, even sometimes allowing a client to rearrange the volume structure on the server by adding directories. The `ftp` utility runs atop TCP, the connection-oriented portion of TCP/IP. As such, before transmitting data, `ftp` establishes a connection between the client and the server and has some error-recovery features. The `ftp` utility is a reliable method of data transmission—if the protocol can't establish a connection, it won't attempt to transmit data.

The base syntax of `ftp` is as follows:

```
ftp [-v] [-n] [-i] [-d] [-g] [-s: filename] [hostname]
```

Table 3.2 lists and describes the arguments in this syntax.

TABLE 3.2	Argument	What It Does
The ftp arguments	-v	Suppresses any display of server responses— rather like setting echo off in DOS batch files.
	-n	Prevents automatic logon when the connection with the server has been established.
	-i	Turns off interactive prompting during file transfers.
	-d	Displays all ftp commands exchanged between client and server. Used for purposes of debugging.
	-g	Prevents the use of wildcard characters in path and file names by disabling the globbing capability (defined in Table 3.3).
	-s: *filename*	Specifies a text file containing ftp commands and then runs the commands within the file, similar to running a batch file.
	hostname	Specifies the host to connect to and must be the last parameter specified.

Once the ftp session has been established, you can use the commands listed in Table 3.3 to copy and move files.

TABLE 3.3	Command	Function
The ftp commands	!	Runs the specified command on the local computer, instead of the remote one. Unless otherwise specified, all commands take place on the remote computer.
	?	Describes all ftp commands. Identical in function to help.
	append	Appends a local file to a file on the remote computer, using the current file type setting.

T A B L E 3.3 *(cont.)*	Command	Function
The ftp commands	ascii	Transfers the specified file as an ASCII file (text only). This is the default.
	bell	Toggles on and off a bell to ring after each successful file transfer. By default, the bell is off.
	binary	Transfers the specified file as a binary file.
	bye	Ends the ftp session and exits ftp. Equivalent to quit.
	cd	Moves to a new working directory.
	debug	Toggles debugging. When it's on, all commands sent between the client and server are displayed. By default, it's off.
	delete	Deletes the specified file.
	dir	Displays a list of the working directory's files and subdirectories.
	disconnect	Disconnects from the remote host but keeps ftp active.
	get	Copies a file from the remote host to the local machine, using the current file transfer settings.
	glob	Toggles the use of wildcards in file and directory names (called *globbing*). By default, globbing is on.
	hash	Toggles the display of a hash mark (#) for each 2048-byte block transferred between client and server. By default, hashing is off.
	help	Describes all ftp commands. Identical in function to ?.
	lcd	Changes the working directory on the local host.

T A B L E 3.3 *(cont.)* The ftp commands	**Command**	**Function**
	literal	Sends all comments verbatim to the remote host, expecting a single ftp response in return. Equivalent to quote.
	mdelete	Deletes files on remote hosts (like delete), but allows you to specify more than one file.
	mdir	Displays a list of the remote directory's files and subdirectories. Like ls, except that this command allows you to specify multiple files.
	mget	Copies multiple files from the remote host to the local machine. Similar to get, except permits you to specify more than one file.
	mkdir	Creates a directory on the remote host.
	mls	Returns an abbreviated list of the current directory's files and subdirectories.
	mput	Copies multiple files from the local machines to the remote host. Similar to put, except permits you to specify more than one file.
	open	Connects to the specified ftp server.
	prompt	Toggles prompting, which is on by default during mget and mput operations so that you can okay each file that you're moving. By default, prompting is on.
	put	Copies a local file to the remote host using the current file transfer type. Equivalent to send.
	pwd	Displays the current directory on the remote host.
	quit	Ends the ftp session and disconnects from the remote host. Equivalent to bye.

TABLE 3.3 *(cont.)* The ftp commands	Command	Function
	quote	Sends all comments verbatim to the remote host, expecting a single ftp response in return. Equivalent to literal.
	recv	Copies a file to the local host. Equivalent to get.
	remotehelp	Displays help for remote commands only.
	rename	Renames the specified remote file.
	rmdir	Deletes the specified remote directory.
	send	Copies a local file to the remote host using the current file transfer type. Equivalent to put.
	status	Displays the current status of ftp sessions and which toggled commands are currently active.
	trace	Toggles packet tracing, showing the route of each packet transmitted when running an ftp command.
	type	Sets or displays the current file transfer type (ASCII or binary).
	user	Specifies a user to the remote host.
	verbose	Toggles verbose mode on and off (on by default) so that as file transfers complete, statistics about the efficiency of the file transfer are displayed.

lpr

As described in Unit 2, lpr is the utility used to send print jobs to a TCP/IP printer via a host running lpd, the line printer daemon. To use this utility, you must have previously installed the TCP/IP Print Services on Windows NT Server. The command syntax (explained in Table 3.4) is as follows:

```
lpr -SServer -PPrinter [-oOptions] [-CClass] [-JJobname] [-o
option] [-x] [-d] filename
```

TABLE 3.4	Argument	What It Does
The arguments for lpr	-SServer	Identifies the host with the printer attached to it.
	-PPrinter	Identifies the printer attached to the host.
	-CClass	Specifies the content of the banner page.
	-JJobname	Specifies the name of the print job.
	-o option	Indicates the type of file (by default, assumed to be a text file) to be printed.
	-x	Indicates compatibility with SunOS version 4.x and later.
	-d	Sends the data files before the control file.
	filename	Specifies the name of the file being printed.

When sending PostScript files to a TCP/IP printer, use the -o1 parameter to tell the printer to accept the file "as is" with no processing by the lpdsvc daemon required.

rcp

This utility is used to copy files between a Windows NT computer running rcp and a Unix host running rshd (the rsh daemon). It can also be used from the Windows NT computer to copy files between two Unix hosts running rshd, if those hosts support rcp. The rcp syntax is as follows:

```
rcp [-a | -b] [-h] [-r] source1 source2 ... sourceN
destination
```

Table 3.5 lists and describes the arguments for rcp.

	Argument	What It Does
T A B L E 3.5 The arguments for `rcp`	`-a`	Specifies that the file to be copied is an ASCII file, converting carriage return and linefeed codes to carriage returns on outgoing files, and vice versa on incoming files. This is the default transfer mode.
	`-b`	Specifies that the file to be copied is a binary file. No conversion takes place.
	`-h`	Transfers files with the hidden attribute from the Windows NT computer. If you don't use this switch, the hidden files are not copied.
	`-r`	Recursively copies all contents of all subdirectories from the source to the destination.
	`sourceN`	The source(s) of the files to be copied.
	`destination`	The destination of the files to be copied. If more than one source is specified, the destination must be a directory; otherwise, only the last file specified will be copied.

Files cannot be copied onto themselves with `rcp`. You can't replace a file with another file of the same name.

When specifying a source, you can either specify the name of the host and the user doing the copying (as `hostname.christa`) or omit them. If you omit the host name and user name, they're assumed to be that of the local host and the person logged on. Also, if you use a fully qualified domain name to identify the host (as *hostname.hostname.domain*), you must specify the user name; if you do not, the user name will be assumed to be the last item after the final period.

If you're copying files from one remote host to another from a Windows NT machine, you must specify the host name or IP address.

When specifying directories, remember that the default is the working directory. Unless you begin the file name with a backward slash to indicate another directory (assuming that you're running the command from a Windows NT machine) or a period (to indicate the current directory), the source is assumed to be relative to the working directory.

rexec

This utility runs specified noninteractive Unix commands on a remote host running the rexc service. Its syntax is as follows:

```
rexec host [-1 username] [-n] command
```

Table 3.6 lists and describes the arguments for rexec.

TABLE 3.6	Argument	What it Is/Does
The arguments for rexec	host	The name of the remote host on which to run the command.
	-1 username	The user's name on the remote host.
	-n	Redirects the input to NUL, instead of to the remote command as is done by default.
	command	The command to be run.

The rexec utility will not run most interactive commands. To run them, use telnet (discussed in a later section).

rsh

Like rexec, rsh runs specified noninteractive Unix commands on a remote host running the corresponding service. Its syntax is as follows:

```
rsh host[-l username] [-n] command
```

Table 3.7 lists and describes the arguments for rexec.

TABLE 3.7	Argument	What It Is/Does
The arguments for rsh	host	The name of the remote host on which to run the command.
	-l username	The user's name on the remote host. If you omit it, the name of the logged-on user is used.
	-n	Redirects the input to NUL, instead of to the remote command as is done by default.
	command	The command to run.

Unlike rexec, rsh requires that you supply a user name in order to use the utility. Thus, if you're logged on to a Windows NT domain, the domain controller must be up and running so that it can supply your user name to the remote host.

telnet

This terminal emulation utility allows you to run interactive commands on a specified remote host that is running the telnet service. It's based on TCP and, therefore, is connection oriented. No data can pass between server and client until the connection is established, and if it should break, telnet will inform you.

Windows NT comes with a Telnet application, located in the Accessories program group, or you can start `telnet` from the command prompt. To connect to a remote host, you must specify the name or IP address of the remote host. You can supply a port on the remote host to connect to, but if you do not, the default value is 23.

> The `telnet` utility supports only character-based applications. X-Windows is needed to connect to GUI applications running on a Unix server. At this time, Windows NT does not supply X-Windows, but third-party vendors supply X-Windows connectivity.

tftp

Like `ftp`, the Trivial File Transfer Protocol utility is used to transfer files between a local and a remote host. It's simpler than `ftp` and not as reliable. Unlike `ftp`, which is based on connection-oriented TCP and will not begin transferring data until a connection has been established, `tftp` is based on the connectionless UDP and does not establish a connection before sending datagrams. It also differs from `ftp` in that it does not supply user authentication in the form of a logon name and password, but relies instead on Unix read and write permissions to protect data—that is, when using the `put` command, the user must have permission to write files to the remote host. Its syntax is as follows:

```
tftp [-i] host [get | put] source [destination]
```

Table 3.8 lists and describes the arguments for `tftp`.

T A B L E 3.8 The arguments for `tftp`	Argument	What It Is/Does
	-I	Specifies that the file to be transferred is binary, not text (the default).
	host	The name of the source host, whether it be remote or local.

T A B L E 3.8 *(cont.)*	Argument	What It Is/Does
The arguments for tftp	get or put	States whether the user is copying a file *from* the remote host (get) or copying it *to* the remote host (put).
	source	The file to be copied.
	destination	Specifies where to put the file.

Configuring RAS and Dial-Up Networking with TCP/IP

Windows NT comes with two related services:

- Remote Access Service (RAS) server product, which allows users to dial in

- Dial-Up-Networking (DUN), which allows users to dial out, perhaps to reach the Internet

You can't configure DUN for outgoing calls unless RAS is set to permit outgoing calls.

Configuring RAS for Use with TCP/IP

With RAS installed on the Windows NT machine, clients can dial in to the server and access the network, connecting just as though their network connection was via the local network instead of via telephone line. The mechanics of installing RAS are not really relevant here; instead, we'll concentrate on what needs to be done to set up RAS for use with TCP/IP.

You need to set up TCP/IP on the RAS server for two reasons:

- To identify it as a host on the local network

- To supply an IP address to RAS clients

The first part is covered in setting up TCP/IP as described in Unit 2. You can configure an IP address to RAS clients during RAS Setup.

If you have TCP/IP already installed when you install RAS, you'll be prompted to configure TCP/IP settings (see Figure 3.1) during the RAS installation.

FIGURE 3.1

Configuring RAS to use TCP/IP

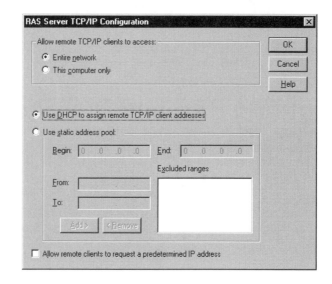

Fill out the dialog box as follows:

- Indicate whether clients should be permitted to access the entire network (the default) or only this computer.

To permit RAS clients to access part of the network, permit access to the entire network and disable TCP/IP bindings on any parts you don't want them to be able to reach.

- Specify whether you want RAS clients to use DHCP (the default) or choose IP addresses from a static address pool. If you check the box in the bottom left of the dialog box, you can permit dial-up clients to request a predetermined IP address.

Be sure that the range you provide does not overlap any preassigned addresses or the addresses in a DHCP scope.

Configuring Dial-Up Networking for Use with TCP/IP

If you install RAS, DUN is automatically installed. (If you try to use DUN first, you'll be prompted to install the service.) The details of how to install DUN aren't important here; let's skip to how to set up the software for use with TCP/IP.

New connections will be set up for use with TCP/IP by default if the protocol is installed.

To set up a connection to use TCP/IP, edit the connection's properties and select the Server tab (see Figure 3.2).

FIGURE 3.2

Setting server proper-
ties for a connection

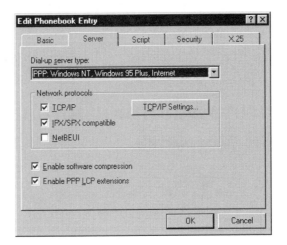

Choose the appropriate dial-up server type (most often PPP, although you may have to use SLIP if you're connecting to a Unix host), and then click TCP/IP Settings to configure the IP addresses you'll be using (see Figure 3.3).

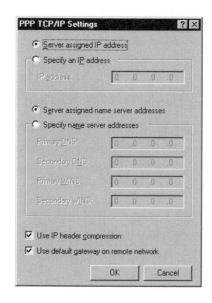

Fill in the addresses as needed. If you're connecting to the Internet or to a local network using DHCP, you can let the server assign you an IP address. The question of whether you must identify your own name server depends on your network—Internet connections typically require you to enter the IP addresses of a primary and secondary name server.

Configuring Multiple-Domain Browsing in a Routed Network

In a Windows NT network, lists of network resources are maintained on a computer known as the *master browser*, helped by computers known as *backup browsers*. The master browser finds out about network resources through broadcasts—when a new machine logs on to the domain, it announces its presence to the master browser. The master browser notes the addition and tells the backup browsers about it. The resource lists on the master browser and backup browsers are periodically updated.

This is a simplistic view of browsing, but it gets the idea across and is adequate for our purposes here.

When a domain consists of a single subnet, this is fine. However, when the domain extends across multiple subnets, this scheme runs into a snag: Routers don't route broadcast messages. They can route directed broadcasts to other subnets, but limited broadcasts sent to 255.255.255.255 (assuming that it's a Class C network) will remain in their subnet. If the master browser is located on subnet A, a new printer on subnet B will never appear in its browse list, because the printer server's "I'm here!" announcements will not make it past the router.

Therefore, unless you want to limit users to browsing their own subnets and no further, you need some way of forwarding those broadcasts beyond their originating segment. To accomplish this and to organize network resources, you must take the master browser and backup browsers and add a third player to the list: the *domain master browser*. The role of the domain master browser is to collate the resources listed by each domain's master browser and present a unified view of what resources are available where (see Figure 3.4).

A domain master browser must be the primary domain controller (PDC) of its domain, whereas a master browser can run Windows NT Server or Workstation, Windows 95, or Windows for Workgroups 3.11b.

The master browsers for each segment send a directed datagram (unacknowledged message) to the domain master browser, informing it that they are their segment's master browser and that the domain master browser needs to get a list of its segment's resources. The domain master browser then requests the list from the master browser and merges its own browse list with that of the master browser so that the master browser has a complete browse list. According to Microsoft, this process takes place every 15 minutes. Backup browsers are notified of changes to the browse list as usual; so when a host views the browse list on a backup browser, the host will see a list of all network resources, whether on its segment or not.

F I G U R E 3.4

Each master browser notifies the domain master browser of its existence and supplies it with a copy of its browse list to merge with that of the others; the domain master browser then supplies each master browser with a copy of the merged browse lists.

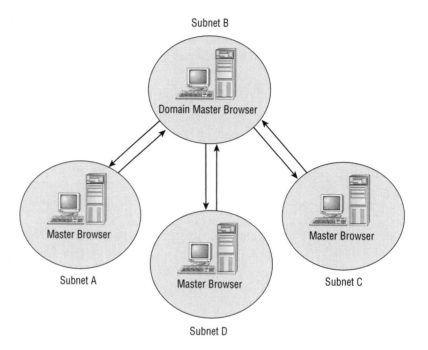

Subnet B

Domain Master Browser

Master Browser

Subnet A

Master Browser

Subnet D

Master Browser

Subnet C

Although workgroups also use master browsers and backup browsers, they cannot follow the domain master browser model as workgroups end at the router. If a workgroup is divided into two subnets, it will become two workgroups with the same name.

Microsoft suggests three alternative methods to set up cross-router browsing:

- WINS
- LMHOSTS
- UDP Port 137

Cross-Domain Routing with WINS

As described in Unit 2, WINS resolves NetBIOS names with IP addresses so that datagrams can be sent to the targeted computer. Thus, when a computer wants to send a message to another computer, the name is resolved to an IP address, which can then be routed or not routed as required. For this to work, Windows NT machines must be part of the domain, and other machines (which cannot be members of a domain as they cannot participate in domain security) must be part of a workgroup with the same name as the domain.

Cross-Domain Routing with LMHOSTS

If WINS is not installed on the network, the second option open to you is to map NetBIOS names to IP addresses with an LMHOSTS file stored in the \System32\drivers\etc directory of each machine. This file must contain all name-to-address mappings for computers not on the local segment (and thus unreachable by limited broadcast).

For master browsers and the domain master browser to communicate, you must include the names and IP addresses of all browsers (backup, master, and domain master) in the LMHOSTS file, as well as the PDC for each domain. The LMHOSTS files for each segment's master browser must also contain the IP address and NetBIOS name of the domain master browser and its domain, and the information must be preloaded into the cache. Thus, a sample entry might look like this:

```
12      PDCName     #PRE        #DOM:BigDomain
```

Any entries preloaded into the name cache should be located at the end of the LMHOSTS file.

Cross-Domain Routing with UDP Port 137

Most routers cannot forward broadcasts, but a few can be configured to forward some types of broadcasts and filter others. Thus, if the other methods won't work, you can always get a router that will fit the bill.

All NetBIOS over TCP broadcasts are sent to port 137. Routers normally filter these packets because they are sent to the hardware broadcast addresses. However, some routers will forward packets sent to this port. The upshot is that an internetwork connected with these routers will look to its member hosts like one big network segment, and the entire thing will be browsable.

This method of cross-segment browsing will increase network traffic due to broadcast forwarding.

Connecting to a Unix Host

1. The `ftp` utility uses _____, which is a connection-oriented transport protocol.

2. Reliable file transfer capabilities are provided for by the _____ command.

3. What terminal emulator application comes with the TCP/IP services?

_____

4. True or False: Windows NT TCP/IP printing is supported on Unix systems running LPSCHED as the LP scheduler.

5. An `ftp` user is commonly allowed to log on to a public `ftp` server using the name _____.

6. True or False: In a non-DNS network, a Windows NT system and a Unix host must use the same HOSTS file for a TCP/IP application to work properly.

7. True or False: A TCP/IP enabled printer directly attached to the network requires an IP address when installing it into a Windows NT print queue.

8. _____ may be used on a Windows NT system to interactively execute commands on a Unix system.

9. Assuming you have a local script file named `ftpcmds`, give the complete `ftp` command from a Windows NT system to transfer from the Unix system named `sysux01`.

_____

10. Enter the command you'd use to get information about user Julie, logged on to Unix host FATBOY.

_____

11. True or False: You can copy files with the `rcp` utility if the host to which you're connecting is running the `rcp` service.

12. To copy files from one Unix server to another, you'd use the _____ utility.

13. True or False: The `tftp` utility runs atop the connectionless IP protocol and, therefore, does not establish a reliable connection between server and client before beginning transmission.

14. Assume that whatever services you'd need would be present and that you don't want to use terminal emulation. To run a non-interactive command on a Unix host from a Windows NT machine, you could use _____ or

_____.

15. What is the purpose of the RHOSTS file?

_____

_____

16. Define the difference between `telnet` and `rsh`.

_____

_____

17. Which two commands available to `tftp` are also available to `ftp`, and what is their function?

_____

_____

18. Ftp is a file transfer utility. How can you use it to run a batch file called `runonce` on the remote host?

_____

_____

19. What is the defining difference between `rexec` and `rsh`?

_____

Configuring RAS and Dial-Up Networking With TCP/IP

20. True or False: An RAS client can use DNS for host name resolution on the Internet.

21. Dial-up support to a Windows NT server is provided via the
_____ protocol.

22. True or False: While configuring RAS for use with TCP/IP, you can give the RAS clients access to the entire network, to a subset of the network, or to only the RAS server when dialing in.

23. If you don't enable DHCP for RAS clients, what method can they use to get IP addresses?

_____

_____

24. True or False: For best performance, you should specify a range of IP addresses that match the DHCP scope on the RAS server's subnet.

25. True or False: You can specify a DHCP server's address when configuring TCP/IP settings for a DUN connection.

26. Typically, when creating an Internet connection, you'll need to provide primary and secondary IP addresses to a _____ .

27. True or False: TCP/IP is only selected as a protocol for use with DUN if you specify that you're connecting to the Internet.

28. Windows NT supports both PPP and _____.

29. Which RAS setting must be configured for DUN to work at all?

_____

_____

Configuring Multiple-Domain Browsing in a Routed Network

30. What browser role may only be performed by a PDC?

_____

31. List the three browser roles in a Windows NT TCP/IP internetwork.

_____

32. The _____ directive in the LMHOSTS file facilitates domain browsing.

33. True or False: All browser entries in an LMHOSTS file must be preinstalled into the name cache to support browsing across routers.

34. True or False: Network broadcasts can be forwarded through port 33 in some routers.

35. List the three options Microsoft suggests to facilitate cross-router browsing.

_____

_____

36. Microsoft suggests using the _____ name service for browsing a subnetted network.

37. Master browsers are updated by the domain master browser every _____ minutes.

38. Explain what this command is doing, what it's part of, and what kind of machine it's on:

```
192.77.26.5    Godlike    #PRE #DOM:Casseopia
```

_____

39. Your router does not support broadcast forwarding. How can you support browsing across routers if WINS is not installed?

_____

_____

3-1 What is `telnet` used for?

    A. File transfer

    B. Terminal emulation

    C. Browsing

    D. Printing

    E. Troubleshooting

3-2 Which of the following does `ftp` use (choose 2)?

    A. UDP

    B. TCP

    C. ICMP

    D. IP

    E. SNMP

3-3 Select one requirement for a Microsoft client to print to a TCP/IP enabled printer.

    A. Client must have NetBIOS enabled.

    B. Client must have printer defined in HOSTS or LMHOSTS.

    C. Windows NT system with TCP/IP printing must be installed.

    D. Windows NT system must have DNS enabled with printer defined in `PRINTCAP` file.

    E. Windows NT with SNMP installed.

3-4   Which `ftp` command will automatically execute commands from a file?

  A. `ftp -s: filename host`

  B. `ftp -f: filename host`

  C. `ftp filename host | scriptfile`

  D. `ftp filename host > scriptfile`

  E. `ftp /filename`

3-5   Which `ftp` command will suppress prompting during multiple file transfers?

  A. `ftp -s`

  B. `ftp -i`

  C. `ftp -d`

  D. `ftp -v`

  E. `ftp /s`

3-6   What utility must Unix support in order to allow a Windows NT system to print to it?

  A. PRINTD

  B. LPD

  C. LPSCHED

  D. LPR

  E. PRINTQ

3-7 What two pieces of information do you need to create a Windows NT print queue for a Unix printer?

    A. Reserved address in DHCP scope

    B. IP address or host name where printer is connected

    C. Static mapping or LMHOST entry in WINS-enabled networks

    D. Printer name as identified on the host

    E. Printer name in HOSTS file

3-8 If you do not specify a server when using the `rsh` command, what will happen?

    A. The command will not work.

    B. The command will execute on the local host.

    C. The command will execute on the host to which the user is presently logged on.

    D. None of the above.

3-9 Your company has two Unix servers behind a locked door. Both servers are running the `rsh` service. One day, all the network personnel with keys are out of the office (bad planning on *someone's* part), but you need to move a file from one server to another. Assuming that you have network access to the servers, which utility will you use to move the file from your Windows NT computer?

    A. `rcp`

    B. `rexec`

    C. `rsh`

    D. `ftp`

SAMPLE TEST

3-10 The DHCP server on your company's network has a scope containing IP addresses ranging from 197.45.3.27 to 197.45.3.42, excluding addresses 197.45.3.35 to 197.45.3.41. The addresses that your network has range from 197.45.3.0 to 197.45.3.50. If you disable DHCP support in your RAS settings for TCP/IP, what is the largest contiguous block of addresses you could specify to be allocated to RAS clients?

   A. 50

   B. 27

   C. 26

   D. None of the above

UNIT

4

Monitoring and Optimization

Test Objectives: Monitoring and Optimization

▪ Given a scenario, identify which tool to use to monitor TCP/IP traffic.

If you can watch network traffic before problems occur, you'll have a better idea of how to fix things so that the problems never materialize. Windows NT comes with several GUI tools you can use to monitor TCP/IP traffic, thus giving you a better understanding of traffic patterns and how to improve the system. These tools include:

- SNMP (Simple Network Management Protocol), for monitoring current system states and, in some cases, making configuration changes

- Performance Monitor, for tracking trends over time

- Network Monitor, for viewing network status

- Event Viewer, for getting system status reports and troubleshooting performance problems based on error messages

Using SNMP

You use SNMP, the basis of all TCP/IP monitoring in Windows NT, to manage computers and other nodes on a TCP/IP network. With the SNMP service installed, you can do the following:

- Monitor DHCP service

- Monitor and manage WINS

- Monitor protocols related to the Internet Information Server

- Create Performance Monitor counters related to TCP/IP

You can also use SNMP to monitor IPX/SPX networks, but TCP/IP must be the primary protocol in use.

The SNMP monitor collects information from hosts on the network that have software called an *agent* installed. The SNMP monitor can communicate with this agent to get a variety of information, including the following:

- Transport protocol statistics (which we'll be focusing on here)
- Identification of computers on the network
- Data about hardware and software configuration
- Performance and usage statistics for each computer
- Application usage statistics
- Event messages and error messages

Figure 4.1 shows how SNMP communication between manager and agent works. In this simple example, the manager queries the agent (perhaps an HTTP server) to find out how many connections it can support. Receiving this request, the agent retrieves the data and replies to the manager.

FIGURE 4.1

SNMP communication between manager and agent

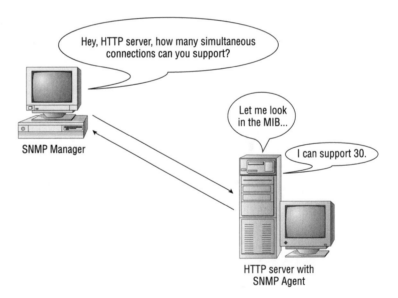

Installing SNMP

After TCP/IP is installed, you can install the SNMP service from the Services tab in Control Panel's Network applet. After you copy the files, you're prompted to configure the service.

1. In the Microsoft SNMP Properties dialog box, select the Agent tab, and supply the name or e-mail address of the person to be contacted and where that person is located. Then, check all the services you want to monitor.

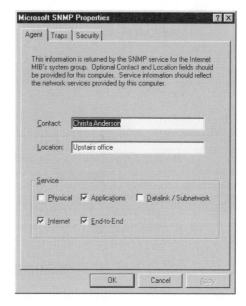

2. Select the Traps tab, and supply the name of the SNMP community to which the node belongs and the IP address of the computer that should receive traps (alerts that a tolerance has been exceeded).

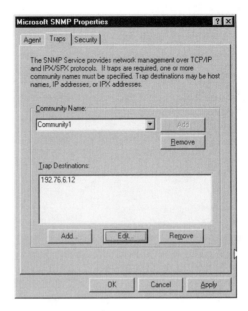

3. Select the Security tab, and list the community names from which this computer should accept SNMP requests for data (public is the default, but for security reasons you probably won't want to use public for your real community name), and supply the IP (or, if applicable, IPX) addresses of the SNMP monitors from which this machine should accept packets.

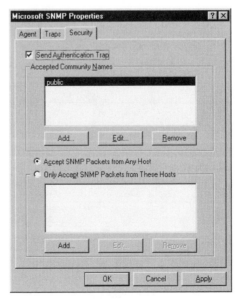

After you install and configure the service, you'll need to reboot the computer. Henceforth, the SNMP service will begin automatically each time the system is booted.

Only the SNMP service is automatically started. The SNMP Trap service, used to hear trap alerts, is set for manual startup and must be initialized from the Services applet in Control Panel or from the command prompt with the NET START command.

To manually start or stop the SNMP service or to change its startup parameters, activate the Services applet in Control Panel. Highlight SNMP in the list of installed services, and click the Start or Stop buttons, or click Startup to modify its startup settings. To configure these settings, you must have Administrator privileges.

The Management Information Base

Each host to be managed has a text file called a *management information base* (MIB) for each element to be monitored. The MIB defines the objects to be monitored with the following information:

- Their syntax
- The access provided to the monitor (read only or read/write)
- Their status (mandatory or not)
- A description of the object

The Windows NT Resource Kit includes a sample MIB (originally from an SNMP mailing list) called TOASTER.MIB to show you the syntax. Here is one object from the MIB:

```
toasterDoneness OBJECT-TYPE
                SYNTAX  INTEGER (1..10)
                ACCESS  read-write
                STATUS  mandatory
                DESCRIPTION
```

```
                                    "This variable controls how well done
ensuing toast

                                    should be on a scale of 1 to 10.
Toast made at 10

                                    is generally considered unfit for
human consumption;

                                    toast made at 1 is lightly warmed."
                        ::= { toaster 4 }
```

Thus, the value associated with toasterDoneness would indicate how well done that toast was. The monitor could then assess whether that value fell within certain tolerances (say, between 3 and 7 for properly done toast) and issue a warning to a network administrator if those tolerances were exceeded. The value in brackets at the bottom of the sample is the number of the object—toasterDoneness is the fourth object type defined in the MIB.

This sample MIB follows a standard called MIB-II. If hardware or software vendors such as Microsoft create a product that they want to be capable of being monitored with SNMP, they must create a MIB following this standard for their product.

When the network administrator needs information about a certain managed object, he or she can request that information from the SNMP monitor. The monitor queries the host for that information, using the object's identifier. The host then looks up the identifier, finds the value associated with it, and reports back to the monitor.

Object Identifiers

Each object defined in a MIB has a unique identifier known as an OID, or object identifier, that identifies not only the object but its category. OIDs are organized in a treelike structure; SNMP OIDs all belong to the `iso.org.dod.internet` branch, represented by the numbers 1.3.6.1. Each additional branch below this main category further identifies the object, using the same dotted format for names or numbers. All in all, the nomenclature works a bit as IP addresses do, with their network portion assigned by the InterNIC and their host portion assigned locally, except that all public MIBs use OIDs that are defined from top to bottom.

The farther down in the branchwork you go, the longer the OID. To return to our TOASTER.MIB example, toasterDoneness would have a MIB of 1.3.6.1.4.1.2.4 (for .iso.org.dod.internet.private.enterprisese .epilogue.toaster.doneness), with a zero appended to specify that you're referring to a specific instance of toasterDoneness. This gets a little long, so some SNMP monitors let you take a shortcut for all MIBs within the iso.org.dod.internet.mgmnt.mib-2 branch, letting you cut off the prefix and use only the object name.

OID names begin with a period unless you're using the abbreviation that permits you to leave off the branch location for MIB-2 OIDs; in that case, you don't use a leading period.

MIBs Related to TCP/IP Traffic

Windows NT's SNMP implementation supports the transport-related MIBs found on the Windows NT Resource Kit CD and described in the following sections.

The ftp, gopher, and http MIBs are all part of monitoring IIS, the Internet Information Server.

The DHCP MIB

The DHCP MIB contains the following information:

- The time at which the server was started
- The number of discovery messages the server has received
- The number of requests for IP addresses the server has received
- The number of messages DHCP clients have sent releasing IP addresses
- The number of offers sent
- The number of acks received
- The number of declined requests
- A list of subnets

- Subnet addresses
- The number of available addresses
- The number of addresses being used

The FTP MIB

The FTP MIB contains the following information:

- The high word (highest 32 bits) of the number of bytes sent by the server
- The low word of the total number of bytes sent by the server
- The high word of the total number of bytes received by the server
- The low word of the total number of bytes received by the server
- The total number of files sent by the server
- The total number of files received by the server
- The number of anonymous users currently logged on to the server
- The number of named users currently logged on to the server
- The number of anonymous users who have ever logged on to the server
- The number of named users who have ever logged on to the server
- The maximum number of anonymous users who have logged on to the server at one time
- The maximum number of named users who have logged on to the ftp server at one time
- The current number of connections to the server
- The maximum number of connections to the server
- The number of connections (successful and unsuccessful) that have been attempted to the server
- The number of logon attempts that have been made to the server

The Gopher MIB

The Gopher MIB contains the following information:

- The high word (highest 32 bits) of the number of bytes sent by the server

- The low word of the number of bytes sent by the server

- The high word of the number of bytes received by the server

- The low word of the number of bytes received by the server

- The total number of files sent by the server

- The total number of directory listings sent by the server

- The total number of searches done by the server

- The current number of anonymous connections to the server

- The current number of named connections to the server

- The total number of anonymous connections ever made to the server

- The total number of named connections ever made to the server

- The current number of connections made to the server

- The maximum number of connections ever made to the server at one time

- The number of connection attempts that have been made to the server

- The number of logon attempts that have been made to the server

- The number of aborted connections that have been made to the server

The HTTP MIB

The HTTP MIB contains the following information:

- The high word (highest 32 bits) of the number of bytes sent by the server

- The low word of the number of bytes sent by the server

- The high word of the number of bytes received by the server

- The low word of the number of bytes received by the server
- The total number of files sent by the server
- The current number of anonymous connections to the server
- The current number of named connections to the server
- The total number of anonymous connections ever made to the server
- The total number of named connections ever made to the server
- The maximum number of anonymous users who have logged on to the server at one time
- The maximum number of named users who have logged on to the server at one time
- The current number of connections to the server
- The maximum number of simultaneous connections to the server
- The number of connection attempts that have been made to the server
- The number of logon attempts that have been made to the server
- The number of GET requests made to the server
- The number of POST requests made to the server
- The number of HEAD requests made to the server
- The number of requests made to the server that are not GET, POST, or HEAD requests
- The number of CGI requests made to the server
- The number of BGI requests made to the server
- The number of requests that the server could not fulfill because the file requested could not be found

The WINS MIB

The WINS MIB contains the following information:

- The time at which the server was started
- The last time that the WINS server was scavenged (old entries released and released entries marked as extinct) automatically

- The last time that the WINS server was scavenged manually
- The last time that extinct entries were removed
- The last time that entries still in use were revalidated
- The last time that automatic replication took place
- The last time that manual replication took place
- The last time that replication took place upon prompting from another WINS server
- The last time that replication took place because a name registration changed
- The last time that an LMHOSTS file was imported into WINS
- The last time that the counters on the WINS server were set to zero
- The number of registrations received
- The number of releases received
- The number of successful (and failed) queries
- The interval (in milliseconds) at which entries are refreshed
- The interval (in milliseconds) at which entries are marked as extinct
- The interval (in milliseconds) at which extinct entries are discarded
- The low word (lowest 32 bits) of the version counter that WINS should use
- The high word (highest 32 bits) of the version counter that WINS should use
- A variable determining whether the server should be able to replicate with machines other than its pull and push partners
- A variable determining whether static data being imported should be read in at initialization and reconfiguration time
- A variable determining whether logging is to be done
- The paths to the log file and to the backup directory

- A variable determining whether WINS should back up when the service is stopped (only applicable if a path to the backup directory is specified)

- A variable determining whether static records should be treated as dynamic records in the case of an address conflict

- A list of data files used for static initialization of the WINS database, and the name of the data file to use

- Entries in the Datafiles table and an index for them

- A variable determining whether a pull should be done at initialization time

- A variable determining the maximum number of retries to be attempted if a pull operation fails

- A list of pull partners

- Data corresponding to each pull partner, including the number of retries to be attempted, the partner's IP address, the number of replications, and others

- The address of the remote pull partner

- The time at which pull replication should occur

- The time interval for pull replication

- The precedence for special groups defined in WINS

- The number of times that replication was successful since the counters were reset to zero

- The number of times that replication was unsuccessful (due to communication failures) since the counters were reset to zero

- The low and high words of the version number of records found in the WINS

- A variable determining whether a push should be done at system initialization

- A variable determining whether a push should be done when an address changes

- A list of push partners for the server

- The address of the push partner
- A variable determining how many updates should provoke a push
- A place to enter an IP address to force the WINS server to initiate a pull session with the specified server (and one to do this for a push session)
- A place to enter an IP address to delete all WINS information for a remote WINS server (cannot be used to delete information on the managed server)
- A variable to cause WINS to scavenge
- A variable that can specify a file of static mappings that WINS should import
- A variable setting the number of worker threads in WINS
- A variable that sets the priority class of the WINS process to normal or to high
- A command to reset counters to zero
- A place to enter an IP address to delete all WINS data for a remote WINS server
- A place to enter an IP address to retrieve data from a remote WINS server
- An object containing the WINS database (cached)
- Data pertaining to records in the database, including their address, version, and state (active, released, or extinct)
- The high and low words of the WINS version for the counter

 The Windows NT Server Resource Kit includes a utility, PERF2MIB.EXE, with which you can build new MIBs.

If you read through these last sections, you noticed something significant. You can monitor information for all these MIB types, but you can remotely *manage* only one: WINS. You can set the WINS objects that have read/write permission either with the Registry Editor or with SNMP.

Agents and Managers

In the "Management Information Base" section, I mentioned that the SNMP monitor could request information about an object if that object were defined in a MIB. That's half the story. The other half is the *agent*, the software that the host requires in order to read the MIB and communicate with the monitor. Windows NT (both Server and Workstation) supplies an agent in the form of the optional SNMP service, which must be installed on every host that is to be managed.

SNMP Agent Configuration

By default, SNMP agents are configured to receive messages through port 161 and hear traps through port 162. If you need to install more than one SNMP agent, you can edit the port assignments for one in the SERVICES file (no extension, but you can open it with Notepad) found in `System32\ Drivers\Etc`. Find the entries that look like this:

```
snmp              161/udp    snmp
snmp-trap         162/udp    snmp
```

The first column describes the service for which the port was assigned, the second, the port number, the third, the protocol used, and the fourth, the service alias.

Although you must install TCP/IP before installing the SNMP service, SNMP does not use TCP/IP to send messages, but rather User Datagram Protocol (UDP). When you install TCP/IP, you're in fact installing the TCP/IP suite of protocols, of which one is UDP.

When the SNMP service is running on your Windows NT computer, it waits for a datagram requesting information from the SNMP manager. When it receives such a message, it performs one of the following operations:

`get` retrieves a specific value for a managed object.

`get next` retrieves the next value in the MIB.

`set` changes the value of a managed object with read/write privileges.

All these operations are performed only in response to a request from the SNMP manager. The SNMP agent will only send unrequested messages when the node is stopped or started or when certain tolerances are exceeded. These alerts are called *traps* and are sent to the IP address, IPX address, or host name that you supplied when setting up the SNMP service on that machine.

When the SNMP manager receives the data from the agent, it may either display it or save in a database for future reference.

SNMP Monitors and Managers

Windows NT itself does not come with an SNMP manager, but the Windows NT Server Resource Kit (available for purchase separately or as part of the TechNet subscription) includes SNMPMon, an SNMP monitoring tool, and SNMPUtil, a managing utility.

SNMPMon   SNMPMon is found in the Diagnostics section of the Resource Kit folder available from the Start menu and keeps a running tally of SNMP functions performed, including:

- The number of nodes being monitored
- The number of queries made since the service was started
- The number of command lines executed since the service was started
- The number of records written to the database

This information is displayed in a small dialog box and dynamically updated.

SNMPMon isn't limited to monitoring SNMP traffic, however. As implied by the fourth option, it can also log the collected statistics to an ODBC database for future reference. This logging can be done for either all queries or only those within certain thresholds (either edge or level triggered).

> If an event is logged when a condition is met, it is said to be level triggered; if logged when it is not met, it is said to be edge triggered.

SNMPMon can also be used for basic management tasks, executing simple commands based on the information returned as specified in a configuration file, including:

- Whether an agent responds to a query

- Whether the agent is able to respond to the query as requested, based on whether it supports the requested variable

- Whether the value with which it responded was greater than, less than, or equal to the expected value

A *configuration file* is an ASCII text file containing one or more monitored node descriptions, consisting of a scope declaration followed by one or more conditional statements. A *scope declaration* identifies the agent to be queried and the MIB object to be monitored and specifies whether logging is to be done and under what conditions. Optionally, a scope declaration can identify the database in which retrieved information is to be recorded, including the name of the table, user ID, and any password required to access the database. The syntax for a scope declaration looks like this:

```
<Node ID> <OID> <Poll interval> <Default log setting> [<ODBC
data source> <ODBC table name> <ODBC user ID> [<ODBC
password>]]
```

Table 4.1 explains this syntax, and Table 4.2 describes the optional settings for data logging.

TABLE 4.1 The scope declaration syntax	Syntax	What It Is/Does
	Node ID	Identifies the computer being monitored, whether by computer name, IP address, or a text file listing all computers
	OID	The MIB object identifier
	Poll interval	Describes (in seconds) the interval at which this computer should be monitored
	Default log setting	Can be set either to zero (do not log) or to 1 (log if one of the conditions described below is set)

TABLE 4.2	Syntax	What It Does/Is
The optional settings for data logging	ODBC data source	Names the database in which the logged data should be recorded
	ODBC table name	Identifies the specific table within the database into which to record the data
	ODBC user ID	The user ID for that database
	ODBC password	The password, if any required, for the database

WARNING

Be careful when entering the name of the table into which you're recording the data. If the named table does not exist, it will be created. A typographical error could result in "lost" data because you won't find it in the table where you expected it.

Each scope description is followed by one or more conditional statements, based on which data is logged. The conditional statements follow this syntax:

```
<Condition> <Log trigger> [<Command-line trigger> <Command-
line timeout> <Command line>]
```

Table 4.3 explains this syntax, and Table 4.4 describes the possible values for Condition.

TABLE 4.3	Syntax	What It Does/Is
The syntax of conditional statements	Condition	Describes the circumstance being logged. This value may be any of the values in Table 4.4.
	Log trigger	Describes what should happen when a condition is met, whether the event should not be logged (0), logged if the condition is not met (1), or logged when the condition is met (2).

T A B L E 4.3 (cont.)	Syntax	What It Does/Is
The syntax of conditional statements	Command-line trigger	Either zero, to not execute the specified command line when a condition is met, or 1, to execute it.
	Command-line timeout	Describes, in milliseconds, the period given to allow the command line to execute. If a value other than zero is provided, the command line terminates when this timeout is exceeded.
	Command line	The command line to execute when the condition is met.

T A B L E 4.4	Value	Met When...
The possible values for Condition	NO_RESPONSE	The node does not respond to the query
	RESPONDED	The node responds to the query, regardless of the value
	SUPPORTED	The node responds with a valid value from the query
	NOT_SUPPORTED	The node responds, but does not support the value in question
	<x	The result is less than the integer x
	>x	The result is greater than the integer x
	=x	The result is equal to the integer x

A configuration file can contain more than one conditional, but as soon as the first conditional statement is satisfied, no more conditionals are executed. You can't set up a string of conditionals to monitor all at once.

Each monitored node description is separated by a blank line or by a C++ comment character. You can use comments to introduce these descriptions, but you can't include comments within a scope declaration or conditional statement. After you create the file, save it as type.INI.

If you don't use spaces in the name of your configuration file, you won't have to enclose it in quotation marks to use it. Configuration files are always run from the command line.

If you run SNMPMon from the Start menu, all you get is the little dialog box showing queries and so forth, as described previously. To get SNMPMon to work with a configuration file, you must run it from the command line, like this:

```
snmpmon configuration_file
```

In this command, configuration_file is the name of the text file with the monitored node descriptions. Be sure to include the full path if the file isn't in the path.

SNMPMon assumes that all community names are "public." You can't change the community name in this version of the utility. You also can't adjust the amount of time allocated for agents to respond to queries; you must use the preset value of 750ms and two retries in case of timeout.

SNMPUtil   SNMPUtil is a browsing tool meant to collect information about a specified node, such as the hardware installed or the services running. It uses the following syntax:

```
snmputil {{get | getnext | walk} agent community oid [oid] |
trap}
```

Table 4.5 explains this syntax.

TABLE 4.5	Syntax	What It Does
The syntax that SNMPUtil uses	get	Retrieves the value of the current OID
	getnext	Retrieves the value of the MIB following the object specified by OID
	walk	Retrieves all the values of the portion of the MIB specified by OID
	agent	Specifies the computer to query, identifying it by IP address or hostname (if the hostname is mapped to an IP address in a local HOSTS file or in a DNS server)
	community	Specifies the community name*
	oid	Specifies the object identifier of the object being queried, either in numeric format or in words
	trap	Tells SNMPUTIL to listen for and trap protocol data units (PDUs)

*All valid community names are listed in the SNMP Properties dialog box accessible from the Network applet in Control Panel.

SNMP Security

Agents may not want to send data to all SNMP managers. You can edit the SNMP security options from the service's Properties dialog box (see Figure 4.2).

SNMP security is based on the concept of *communities*, logical arrangements of SNMP machines organized under a common name, like a workgroup. Like a workgroup, members of a community are often physically proximate, but they don't have to be. Nor does the membership of the community have to bear any relationship to the membership of the workgroup or domain to which the computers belong. Essentially, the name of the community is a password and should be treated as such.

FIGURE 4.2

Configuring SNMP
security

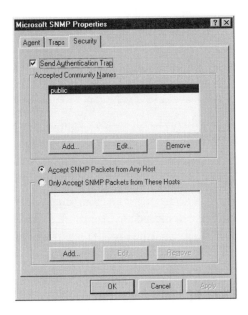

Only agents and managers that are part of the same community can talk to one another. By default, all SNMP Windows NT machines are originally part of the *public* community. For added security, you may want to remove this community name or create another community. Notice the Send Authentication Trap checkbox at the top of the Properties dialog box shown in Figure 4.2. When this checkbox is checked (as it is by default), if an SNMP machine from a community to which this machine does not belong attempts to communicate with this machine, it sends a trap to the machine listed on the Traps tab, recording the failed access.

An SNMP machine may be a member of more than one community.

To edit the list of communities from which an SNMP agent will accept requests, select the Security tab of the SNMP Properties dialog box.

- To add a community, click the Add button and type the name of the community in the dialog box that appears.

- To edit a community's name, click the Edit button and retype the name as necessary.

- To delete a community from the list, select it and click the Remove button.

When you remove a community name, the change takes place immediately—you won't be prompted for confirmation—and the only way to reverse it is to click the dialog box's Cancel button.

If an SNMP machine does not belong to any community, this is the same as having a device that is not password-protected—*any* SNMP machine can communicate with it, regardless of its community membership.

The Performance Monitor

The Performance Monitor (in the Administrative Tools [Common] folder), shown in Figure 4.3, is a tool you can use to monitor an extensive array of counters relating to just about every aspect of your system: disk, memory, processor, cache, redirector, and more.

FIGURE 4.3

Performance Monitor interface for adding counters

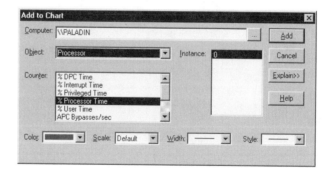

When you install TCP/IP on your computer and make it the default transport protocol, you add some new performance counters to the Performance Monitor, relating to TCP/IP performance. Those counters are listed in Table 4.6.

Category	Description
FTP Service	Connection and file transfer statistics
ICMP	Send and receive rates for Internet Control Message Protocol (ICMP) messages, and error counts for this protocol
IP	Send and receive rates for Internet Protocol (IP) datagrams, and error counts for this protocol
Network Interface	The rate at which bytes and packets are sent over a TCP/IP network connection
TCP	Send and receive rates for Transmission Control Protocol (TCP) segments, and the number of TCP connections for each of the possible connection states
UDP	Send and receive rates for User Datagram Protocol (UDP) datagrams, and error counts for this protocol
WINS Service	Rates at which queries, conflicts, renewals, registrations, and releases occur

Each of these categories has individual counters that you can monitor to watch network activity. The following sections will explain the counters in each category. You don't have to memorize all the counters for each category, but you should have a good idea of what kind of data each object monitors.

You don't have to monitor all the counters in a given category—in fact, you'll probably be swamped with data if you do. Instead, concentrate on getting the information that *you* need.

ftp Service

The ftp service included with TCP/IP provides file transfer services to its clients. The information important to ftp performance is related to:

- The rate at which bytes are sent and received
- The number of files sent
- The number of concurrent users
- The maximum number of users
- The types of users

Table 4.7 lists the ftp service counters and explains their role, showing the data you can monitor.

All ftp counters are set to zero every time the service is restarted.

T A B L E 4.7 The ftp Service counters	**Counter**	**Description**	**Further Information**
	Bytes Received/Sec	The number of data bytes received per second.	This count includes only data, not headers or control bytes. This counter is a subset of Bytes Total/Sec.
	Bytes Sent/Sec	The number of data bytes sent per second.	This count includes only data, not headers or control bytes. This counter is a subset of Bytes Total/Sec.

	Counter	Description	Further Information
T A B L E 4.7 *(cont.)* The ftp Service counters	Bytes Total/Sec	The number of data bytes sent and received per second.	This count includes only data, not headers or control bytes. This counter represents the sum of Bytes Sent/Sec and Bytes Received/Sec.
	Connection Attempts	The total number of connections made to the service since it was started, not including those that failed at the TCP or IP level.	This count should either remain constant or increase over time—it's not decremented when a connection is broken.
	Current Anonymous Users	The current number of anonymous users, based on the count at the last time of observation.	Displays current, successful connections only. If an anonymous logon failed and the user made a named logon, it won't be counted here. If anonymous connections are not permitted on this server, the value is always zero.
	Current Connections	The current number of connections, based on the count at the last time of observation.	Displays current connections only.
	Current Non- Anonymous Users	The current number of named users, based on the count at the last time of observation.	Displays current, successful connections only. If an anonymous logon failed and the user made a named logon, it is counted here. If authentication is not required on this server, the value is always zero.

TABLE 4.7 (cont.) The ftp Service counters	**Counter**	**Description**	**Further Information**
	Files Received	The total number of files received by the service since it was started.	This count is a subset of the Files Total counter and should either remain constant or increase over time.
	Files Sent	The total number of files sent by the service since it was started.	This count is a subset of the Files Total counter and should either remain constant or increase over time.
	Files Total	The total number of files sent and received by the service since it was started.	This count is the sum of the Files Sent and Files Received counters. It should either remain constant or increase over time.
	Logon Attempts	The total number of connections to the service since it was started, counting only those in which the users were able to log onto ftp.	This count does not include successful connections but failed logons. To find the number of failed logon attempts, subtract this number from Connection Attempts.
	Maximum Anonymous Users	The maximum number of anonymous users to log on to the service at one time since the service was started.	Applies to current, successful connections only. If an anonymous logon failed and the user made a named logon, it won't be counted here. If anonymous connections are not permitted on this server, the value is always zero.
	Maximum Connections	The maximum number of connections maintained at one time since the service was started.	Displays a value that may not be current.

	Counter	Description	Further Information
TABLE 4.7 *(cont.)* The ftp Service counters	Maximum NonAnonymous Users	The maximum number of named users to log on to the service at one time since the service was started.	Applies to current, successful connections only. If a named logon failed and the user made an anonymous logon, it won't be counted here. If user authentication is not required on this server, the value is always zero.
	Total Anonymous Users	The total number of anonymous users to log on to the service since the service was started.	Applies to successful connections only. If an anonymous logon failed and the user made a named logon, it won't be counted here. If anonymous connections are not permitted on this server, the value is always zero.
	Total Nonanonymous Users	The total number of named users to log on to the service since the service was started.	Applies to successful connections only. If a named logon failed and the user made an anonymous logon, it won't be counted here. If user authentication is not required on this server, the value is always zero.

ICMP Counters

Internet Control Message Protocol (ICMP) is a maintenance protocol that sends messages encapsulated within IP datagrams. It's used to build and maintain routing tables, help with Path Maximum Transfer Unit discovery, diagnose problems, and adjust flow control to prevent link or router saturation.

In its troubleshooting role, ICMP is the protocol used by ping and tracert.

The ICMP performance object measures the rates at which messages are sent and received and monitors protocol errors. Table 4.8 describes the counters used with this performance object.

You must have SNMP installed to use the ICMP performance counters.

TABLE 4.8 ICMP performance counters	Counter	Description	Further Information
	Messages Outbound Errors	The number of messages that were not sent due to a problem within the ICMP protocol.	This count includes only ICMP-related problems, not those related to IP not routing the datagram in which the message was encapsulated.
	Messages Received Errors	The number of messages received but determined to contain errors (bad checksums, for example).	
	Messages Received/Sec	The rate at which messages are received.	Count includes received messages with errors in them. This count is a subset of Messages/Sec.
	Messages Sent/Sec	The rate at which messages are sent.	Count includes messages sent with errors in them. This count is a subset of Messages/Sec.
	Messages/ Sec	The rate at which messages are sent and received.	This count is the sum of Messages Sent/Sec and Messages Received/Sec and includes messages with errors.

T A B L E 4.8 *(cont.)* ICMP performance counters	Counter	Description	Further Information
	Received Address Mask	The number of ICMP Address Mask Request messages received.	
	Received Address Mask Reply	The number of ICMP Address Mask Reply messages received.	
	Received Dest Unreachable	The number of Destination Unreachable messages received.	
	Received Echo Reply/Sec	The rate at which Echo Reply messages are received.	
	Received Echo/Sec	The rate at which Echo messages are received.	
	Received Parameter Problem	The number of Parameter Problem messages received.	
	Received Redirect/Sec	The rate at which Redirect messages are received.	
	Received Source Quench	The number of Source Quench messages received.	
	Received Time Exceeded	The number of Time Exceeded messages received.	
	Received Timestamp Reply/Sec	The rate at which Timestamp Reply messages are received.	

T A B L E 4.8 *(cont.)*	Counter	Description	Further Information
ICMP performance counters	Received Timestamp/ Sec	The rate at which Timestamp messages are received.	
	Sent Address Mask	The number of ICMP Address Mask Request messages sent.	
	Sent Address Mask Reply	The number of ICMP Address Mask Reply messages sent.	
	Sent Dest Unreachable	The number of Destination Unreachable messages sent.	
	Sent Echo Reply/Sec	The rate at which Echo Reply messages are sent.	
	Sent Echo/Sec	The rate at which Echo messages are sent.	
	Sent Parameter Problem	The number of Parameter Problem messages sent.	
	Sent Redirect/Sec	The rate at which Redirect messages are sent.	
	Sent Source Quench	The number of Source Quench messages sent.	
	Sent Time Exceeded	The number of Time Exceeded messages sent.	
	Sent Timestamp Reply/Sec	The rate at which Timestamp Reply messages are sent.	
	Sent Timestamp/Sec	The rate at which Timestamp messages are sent.	

IP Counters

The IP object counters (see Table 4.9) describe errors and the rate at which IP datagrams are sent and received by the computer.

T A B L E 4.9	Counter	Description	Further Information
IP performance counters	Datagrams Forwarded/ Sec	The rate at which the computer received datagrams for which this was not their final destination, and so attempted to forward them.	If the computer is not an IP gateway, this count will only include datagrams successfully source-routed via this computer.
	Datagrams Outbound Discarded	The number of outbound datagrams that were discarded not due to errors, but for other reasons such as a lack of buffer space.	
	Datagrams Outbound No Route	The number of outbound datagrams that were discarded because no route could be found to transmit them to their destination.	
	Datagrams Received Address Errors	The number of received datagrams discarded because the IP address in the destination field was invalid for some reason.	For computers that are not IP gateways, this count will include all datagrams discarded because the destination address was not on the local subnet.
	Datagrams Received Delivered/Sec	The rate at which received datagrams are successfully delivered to IP protocols, such as ICMP.	

TABLE 4.9 *(cont.)*	Counter	Description	Further Information
IP performance counters	Datagrams Received Disarded/Sec	The rate at which received datagrams are discarded not due to errors, but for other reasons such as lack of buffer space.	
	Datagrams Received Header Errors	The number of received datagrams discarded due to errors in their IP headers.	
	Datagrams Received Unknown Protocol	The number of received datagrams discarded because of an unknown or unsupported protocol.	
	Datagrams Received/Sec	The rate at which datagrams are received, including those with errors.	This counter is a subset of Datagrams/Sec.
	Datagrams Sent/Sec	The rate at which datagrams are supplied to IP for transmission by IP protocols such as ICMP.	This counter is a subset of Datagrams/Sec. On IP gateways, it does not include datagrams forwarded to another subnet.
	Datagrams/ Sec	The rate at which datagrams are supplied to IP for sending and receiving, not counting any forwarded datagrams.	This counter is the sum of Datagrams Received/Sec and Datagrams Sent/Sec.
	Fragment Reassembly Failures	Failures detected by the IP reassembly algorithm for any reason.	This is not necessarily a count of discarded IP fragments. Because some algorithms combine fragments as they're received, an accurate count is lost.

TABLE 4.9 *(cont.)*	Counter	Description	Further Information
IP performance counters	Fragmentation Failures	The number of IP datagrams that needed to be fragmented but could not be for some reason.	
	Fragmented Datagrams/ Sec	The rate at which datagrams are successfully fragmented.	
	Fragments Created/Sec	The rate at which datagram fragments are created.	
	Fragments Reassembled/Sec	The rate at which datagram fragments are reassembled.	
	Fragments Received/Sec	The rate at which datagram fragments needing to be reassembled are received.	

Network Interface Counters

The network interface counters (see Table 4.10) collect data for transmission of packets over a TCP/IP network, including transmission errors. These counters may be used on any of four instances of the network interface object (see Figure 4.4).

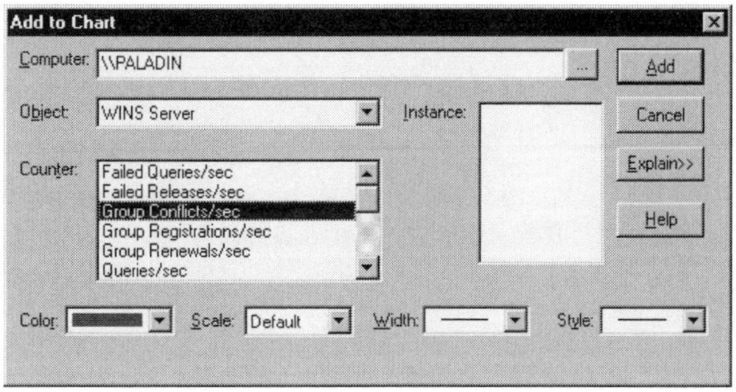

FIGURE 4.4

Instances of the Network Interface object

Instance 1 of the network interface object represents the loopback adapter. Instances 2–4 represent installed network adapters; so be sure that you're looking at the right instance.

	Counter	Description	Further Information
T A B L E 4.10 Network Interface counters	Bytes Received/Sec	The rate at which bytes, including framing characters, are received over each adapter.	This counter is a subset of Bytes Total/Sec.
	Bytes Sent/Sec	The rate at which bytes, including framing characters, are sent over each adapter.	This counter is a subset of Bytes Total/Sec.
	Bytes Total/Sec	The rate at which bytes, including framing characters, are sent and received over each adapter.	This counter is the sum of Bytes Received/Sec and Bytes Sent/Sec.
	Current Bandwidth	An estimate of the total bandwidth currently available, measured in bits per second.	For interfaces that do not vary in bandwidth or for those for which an accurate estimate cannot be made, this is the same as the card's nominal bandwidth (for example, 100Mbps).
	Output Queue Length	The number of packets waiting to be transmitted.	If this number is greater than 2, there's a performance bottleneck. However, as NDIS queues packets, this count will always be zero and is, therefore, not very useful.
	Packets Outbound Discarded	The number of outbound packets discarded not due to errors, but for some other reason (such as inadequate buffer space).	

T A B L E 4.10 *(cont.)*	Counter	Description	Further Information
Network Interface counters	Packets Outbound Errors	The number of outbound packets discarded because of errors.	
	Packets Received Discarded	The number of inbound packets discarded not due to errors, but for some other reason (such as to free buffer space).	
	Packets Received Errors	The number of inbound packets that contained errors that rendered them undeliverable.	
	Packets Received Non-Unicast/Sec	The rate at which subnet broadcast or subnet multicast packets are delivered to a higher-layer protocol for delivery.	
	Packets Received Unicast/Sec	The rate at which unicast packets are delivered to a higher-layer protocol for delivery.	
	Packets Received Unknown	The number of packets received that were discarded due to an unknown or unsupported protocol.	
	Packets Received/Sec	The rate at which packets are received.	This counter is a subset of Packets/Sec.
	Packets Sent Non-Unicast/Sec	The rate at which higher-level protocols submit subnet broadcast or subnet multicast packets for delivery.	

TABLE 4.10 (cont.) Network Interface counters	Counter	Description	Further Information
	Packets Sent Unicast/Sec	The rate at which higher-level protocols submit unicast packets for delivery.	
	Packets Sent/Sec	The rate at which packets are sent.	This counter is a subset of Packets/Sec.
	Packets/Sec	The rate at which packets are sent and received.	This counter is the sum of Packets Received/Sec and Packets Sent/Sec.

TCP Counters

The TCP performance object counters (see Table 4.11) measure the rates at which TCP segments are sent and received using the Transmission Control Protocol and tally the number of TCP connections in each connection state.

The TCP connections states are: CLOSED, SYS-SENT, SYN-RCVD, LISTEN, and CLOSE-WAIT.

TABLE 4.11 TCP performance counters	Counter	Description	Further Information
	Connection Failures	The number of times that a connection has gone straight from SYN-SENT or SYN-RCVD to CLOSED, plus the number of times that a connection has gone straight from LISTEN to SYN-RCVD.	
	Connections Active	The number of times connections have gone straight from SYN-SENT to CLOSED.	

	Counter	Description	Further Information
T A B L E 4.11 *(cont.)* TCP performance counters	Connections Established	Number of connections for which the state is either ESTABLISHED or CLOSE-WAIT.	
	Connections Passive	The number of times connections have gone directly from LISTEN to SYN-RCVD.	
	Connections Reset	The number of times connections have gone straight from either ESTABLISHED or CLOSE-WAIT to CLOSED.	
	Segments Received/Sec	The rate at which segments are received on currently established connections, including segments in error.	This counter is a subset of Segments/Sec.
	Segments Retransmitted/Sec	The rate at which segments are retransmitted.	
	Segments Sent/Sec	The rate at which segments are set on current connections, but excluding retransmissions.	This counter is a subset of Segments/Sec.
	Segments/Sec	The rate at which segments are sent and received with TCP.	This counter represents the sum of Segments Received/Sec and Segments Sent/Sec.

UDP Counters

The UDP performance object counters (see Table 4.12) measure the rate at which datagrams are sent and received using UDP and keep track of errors associated with this protocol.

TABLE 4.12 UDP performance counters	Counter	Description	Further Information
	Datagrams No Port/Sec	The rate at which datagrams are received for which there is no application at the specified port.	
	Datagrams Received Errors	The number of datagrams received that could not be delivered for some reason other than no application at the port.	
	Datagrams Received/Sec	The rate at which UDP datagrams are delivered to UDP users.	This counter is a subset of Datagrams/Sec.
	Datagrams Sent/Sec	The rate at which UDP datagrams are sent from the computer.	This counter is a subset of Datagrams/Sec.
	Datagrams/ Sec	The rate at which UDP datagrams are sent and received.	This counter represents the sum of Datagrams Received/Sec and Datagrams Sent/Sec.

WINS Server Counters

The WINS Server performance object includes counters (see Table 4.13) for monitoring WINS activity and problems: queries, releases, and conflicts.

	Counter	Description	Further Information
T A B L E 4.13 WINS Server perfor- mance counters	Failed Queries/Sec	The rate at which queries are made but not resolved.	Counter is a subset of Queries/Sec.
	Failed Releases/Sec	The rate at which clients attempt to release registra-tions but are unable to do so.	Counter is a subset of Releases/Sec.
	Group Conflicts/Sec	The rate at which group reg-istrations and/or renewals result in conflicts in the WINS database.	Counter is a subset of Total Number of Conflicts/Sec.
	Group Regis-trations/Sec	The rate at which group reg-istrations are received by the WINS server.	Counter is a subset of Total Number of Registrations/Sec.
	Group Renewals/ Sec	The rate at which group renewals are received by the WINS server.	Counter is a subset of Total Renewals/Sec.
	Queries/Sec	The rate at which queries are received by the WINS server.	Counter represents the sum of Failed Queries/Sec and Successful Queries/Sec.
	Releases/Sec	The rate at which releases are received by the WINS server.	Counter represents the sum of Failed Releases/Sec and Successful Releases/Sec.
	Successful Queries/Sec	The rate at which queries are received by the WINS server, and are successful.	Counter is a subset of Queries/Sec.
	Successful Releases/Sec	The rate at which releases are received by the WINS server, and are successful.	Counter is a subset of Releases /Sec.

TABLE 4.13 (cont.)	Counter	Description	Further Information
WINS Server performance counters	Total Number of Conflicts/Sec	The rate at which the WINS server experiences both group and unique conflicts.	Counter represents the sum of Unique Conflicts/Sec and Group Conflicts/Sec.
	Total Number of Registrations/Sec	The rate at which registrations are received by the WINS server.	Counter represents the sum of Unique Registrations/Sec and Group Registrations/Sec.
	Total Number of Renewals/Sec	The rate at which renewals are received by the WINS server.	Counter represents the sum of Unique Renewals/Sec and Group Renewals/Sec.
	Unique Conflicts/Sec	The rate at which unique registrations and./or renewals result in conflicts in the WINS database.	Counter is a subset of Total Number of Conflicts/Sec.
	Unique Registrations/Sec	The rate at which the server receives unique registrations.	Counter is a subset of Total Number of Registrations/Sec.
	Unique Renewals/Sec	The rate at which the server receives unique renewals.	Counter is a subset of Total Renewals/Sec.

The Network Monitor

Integrated with the Performance Monitor is a network-specific tool called the Network Monitor, which you can install using the Services tab in the Network applet in Control Panel. When installed, the utility is accessible from the Administrative Tools (Common) folder. It looks like the dialog box shown in Figure 4.5.

FIGURE 4.5

The Network Monitor is the networking version of Performance Monitor.

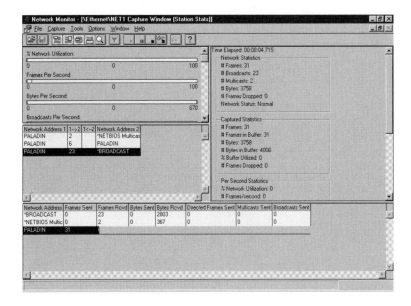

The Network Monitor monitors the data stream on the network (although, for security reasons, it will only display frames and packets for the computer on which it's running) and thus has access to the following information:

- The source and destination addresses of frames

- The headers from each protocol used to send frames

- The data being sent

Capturing Frames

Network Monitor can't do anything until you give it some data to work with. The first step to using it to monitor TCP/IP traffic (or any traffic) is to capture frames on the network. To do so, choose Capture ➤ Start to display a timer in Network Monitor. As packets are grabbed, you'll see the following information displayed, according to sender:

- Frames sent and received

- Bytes sent and received

- Directed frames, broadcasts, and multicasts sent

If you just start capturing frames, you're likely to end up with a lot of data very quickly. Network Monitor can only store as many frames as its buffers can hold, and you're likely to end up with information overload in any case, so you'll want to filter the data according to your needs. In this case, since we're interested in TCP/IP traffic, we'll filter according to protocol. Stop the capture (choose Capture ➤ Stop), and then choose Capture ➤ Filter to open the Capture Filter dialog box:

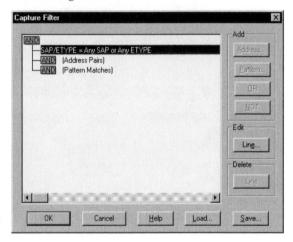

Double-click the SAP/ETYPE branch or click the Line button in the Edit section to edit the protocols observed. You'll see a dialog box like the one in Figure 4.6.

F I G U R E   4.6

Editing protocol filter settings

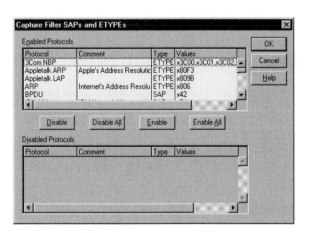

By default, all protocols are enabled. To disable one, double-click it in the list, or highlight it and click the Disable button.

If you want to monitor only a few protocols, it's easiest to disable all of them and then selectively enable the ones you want.

The protocols are arranged in alphabetic order. Notice that there are two instances of IP: one SAP (for service broadcasts) and one ETYPE (for regular traffic). When you've selected all the protocols to monitor, click OK to exit.

To capture only packets sent between certain addresses, edit the Address Pairs line in the Capture Filter dialog box to open the Address Expression dialog box (see Figure 4.7).

F I G U R E 4.7

Editing address pairs

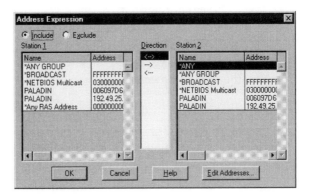

Notice the little arrows between the two columns and how they monitor traffic, either going in only one direction or both ways. Once again, when you've made your choice, exit the dialog box, and the new settings will be displayed in the Capture Filter dialog box.

Finally, if you know the contents of a particular frame that you're looking for, edit the pattern matching settings (see Figure 4.8).

To filter by content, you have to be sure of exactly where the pattern will fall in the frame. The offset is the number of bytes into the frame you expect the pattern to be (in hexadecimal), either from the beginning of the frame or counting from the part of the packet after the network header.

FIGURE 4.8

Filtering by packet
content

 Ethernet packets have a 14-byte header; the size of Token Ring headers
varies.

When choosing pattern types, you have access to the Boolean operators in
the Capture Filter dialog box. Choose combinations of packet content to
make the search as wide or as limited as you like.

When you've created the filter you want, choose Capture ➤ Start to start
the capture process.

The Event Viewer

SNMP is for monitoring the system as a whole and performing some
remote administration, the Performance Monitor is for monitoring rates and
numbers over time, the Network Monitor is for viewing the contents of
traffic sent over the network—what's the Event Viewer for? Essentially, it's
a status check. You can view the records in the Event Viewer (located in the
Administrative Tools (Common) folder) to see whether all TCP/IP services
started properly and, if not, what kinds of errors caused them to fail. If you
find any unexpected behavior in your system, such as the TCP/IP counters
not showing up in the Performance Monitor after you've installed TCP/IP,
you can read the event logs to find out what's happening.

All significant events are noted, not just problems. The Event Viewer records three kinds of events. An *informational event* is significant but requires no action. It is indicated by a blue circle with an *i* in it.

 A *warning event* is a potential problem that may require user action. It is indicated by a yellow circle that contains an exclamation point.

 An *error event* is a problem that caused parts of the system not to function at all. It is indicated by a red Stop sign.

The Event Viewer maintains three logs:

- System

- Application

- Security

For purposes of monitoring TCP/IP, the first two are the logs that concern us.

The System Log

The System log records events noted by Windows NT components, such as services or protocols, for example, a service starting or failing to start.

The Application Log

The Application log records events noted by applications—not necessarily word processors, but also the WINS database, for example, or a failure to open performance counters for TCP/IP because a needed DLL could not be found.

Using SNMP

1. Windows NT includes an agent to allow itself to be monitored, but does not include a(n)

_____ .

2. A(n) _____ destination is the host name or IP address of the SNMP manager application to which you want "events" sent.

3. What does the acronym SNMP stand for?

_____

4. What information do you need to specify the trap destination when configuring SNMP services?

_____

_____

5. The SNMP agent reports significant events, or _____,
to the management application.

6. What SNMP Agent Service should be configured if your Windows NT computer functions as an IP gateway?

_____

7. Where does a Windows NT system send authentication traps?

_____

8. Under what conditions will an SNMP request be rejected by the Windows NT system, even if *Accept SNMP packets from any host* is checked?

_____

9. You want to specify a specific SNMP management application to control/manage your Windows NT system. Where do you specify the community name of this management system?

_____

10. You can use SNMP to monitor several Windows NT services and protocols. Which one(s) can you use it to manage?

_____

11. Network management for a Windows NT system is possible via the _____ agent.

12. All SNMP OIDs begin with the numbers _____.

13. List the required components of a scope identifier with SNMPMon.

_____

_____

14. To get detailed information about a specific node, which utility would you use?

_____

15. Which TCP/IP services can you monitor with SNMP?

_____

_____

16. True or False: Once you install SNMP, by default the SNMP service and SNMP Trap service are automatically started whenever you reboot your system.

17. An event logged when a condition is met is said to be _____
triggered; if logged when a condition is not met, it is said to be
_____ triggered.

18. Identify the two parts of a monitored node description.

_____

_____

19. SNMP agents have_____ and
_____ retries to reply to SNMPMon queries.

20. True or False: SNMPMon recognizes only the _public_ community.

21. Describe what the following SNMPMon statement is doing:

199.46.23.151.3.6.1.5.14.21201

_____

_____

_____

22. Under which Registry subkey are the TCP/IP registry parameter values stored?

_____

23. What two text comments can be entered in the SNMP Agent configuration box?

_____

_____

24. SNMP is used to both monitor and _____ WINS servers on an internetwork.

25. To secure your SNMP agent from unwanted management stations, you should use a community name other than _____.

26. True or False: The IP hostname of the management station must be added to the SNMP agent's HOSTS file in order for the agent to send the management station a trap.

27. True or False: A trap destination IP address must appear in the HOSTS file or be resolved by DNS for SNMP to operate correctly.

28. True or False: When configuring SNMP, the host name of the management application is not case-sensitive, but community names are case-sensitive.

29. SNMP may use a host name to report information to the management application if the host name is defined either in the _____ file or in the _____ database.

30. The _____ protocol is used for management and control of network devices.

The Performance Monitor

31. While monitoring the ICMP performance counters Sent Echo/Second and Received Echo/Second, you notice the Sent counters increasing, while the Received counters remain steady. What TCP/IP application is being monitored, and what is the cause of the problem?

_____

_____

32. True or False: You can use Performance Monitor to track the current number of anonymous FTP connections for problem analysis.

33. What must be installed in order to use Performance Monitor on a WINS server, assuming TCP/IP has already been properly installed and configured?

_____

34. You will find the counter Datagrams Forwarded under the Counter Type
_____ in Performance Monitor.

35. You will find the counter Logon Attempts under the Counter Type
_____ in Performance Monitor.

36. You will find the counter Sent Echo/Second under the Counter Type
_____ in Performance Monitor.

37. You will find the counter Fragment Failures under the Counter Type
_____ in Performance Monitor.

38. PING is monitored by the _____ Performance Monitor Counter Object Type.

39. You will find the counter Connections Established under the Counter Type
_____ in Performance Monitor.

40. You will find the counter Segments/Second under the Counter Type
_____ in Performance Monitor.

41. You will find the counter Current Anonymous Users under the Counter Type
_____ in Performance Monitor.

42. Describe the function of the Network Interface Performance Monitor category.

_____

_____

_____

43. The ftp counters can record two types of users:
_____ and
_____.

44. What is the expected behavior of the Connection Attempts ftp counter?

_____

_____

45. The tracert utility depends on the _____
protocol.

46. True or False: On IP routing Windows NT computers, the IP counters will record datagrams
sent to a subnet other than their own as discarded.

47. The IP category counters keep track of _____ as the
transmission medium.

The Network Monitor

48.   True or False: Network Monitor can capture a packet sent from a TCP/IP client to its own IP address to verify connectivity with the network.

49.   The Network monitors the _____ for the computer on which it's running.

50.   What service must be running for Network Monitor to remotely access another computer's network traffic?

_____

51.   In order to pick up only service broadcast frames, which type of IP protocol would you select?

_____

52.   To capture only selected packets, you must set up a(n)

_____.

53.   True or False: Network Monitor captures only traffic sent to the local server.

54.   Describe how to quickly select only a few protocols to monitor.

_____

_____

_____

55.   The offset for packet content is written in _____.

56.   What is the size of an Ethernet frame's header?

_____

The Event Viewer

57.   List the three types of events the Event Viewer logs.

_____

_____

_____

58.   True or False: The Event Viewer will record an event if the TCP/IP protocol is not loaded at system startup.

59.   If WINS failed to start, you'd look in the _____ log to find out what happened.

60.   True or False: If WINS couldn't load its database, you'd look in the Application log to find out why.

61. Which log would record the failure of a DLL to load if that DLL were necessary for a system service?

_____

62. List the three types of logs maintained by the Event Viewer.

_____

_____

_____

4-1 Which of the following protocol combinations does SNMP use for transport?

    A. WINSOCK over IP

    B. UDP over IP

    C. TCP over IP

    D. TCP over ICMP

    E. UDP over ICMP

4-2 Which Performance Monitor counter charts Fragmentation Failures?

    A. ICMP

    B. FTP

    C. IP

    D. TCP

    E. SNMP

4-3 You want to monitor Datagrams Forwarded in Performance Monitor to evaluate an NT system's overall performance as an IP router. Which protocol must you install?

    A. NetBEUI

    B. NetBIOS Interface

    C. SNMP

    D. ARP

    E. UDP

SAMPLE TEST

4-4   You have noticed a high number of Datagrams Outbound Discarded in Performance Monitor. Of what is this a symptom?

   A. Invalid default gateway

   B. Invalid subnet mask

   C. Lack of buffer space

   D. Invalid physical address

   E. Invalid ARP cache

4-5   Which Performance Monitor counter charts Received Redirect/Sec?

   A. ICMP

   B. FTP

   C. IP

   D. TCP

   E. UDP

4-6   Which Performance Monitor counter charts Datagrams Outbound Discarded?

   A. ICMP

   B. FTP

   C. IP

   D. TCP

   E. UDP

SAMPLE TEST

4-7   Which Performance Monitor counter charts Connections Established?

 A. ICMP

 B. FTP

 C. IP

 D. TCP

 E. SNMP

4-8   Which Performance Monitor counter charts Connections Reset?

 A. ICMP

 B. FTP

 C. IP

 D. TCP

 E. UDP

4-9   Which Performance Monitor counter charts Datagrams Forwarded/Second?

 A. ICMP

 B. FTP

 C. IP

 D. TCP

 E. SNMP

4-10   Which Performance Monitor counter charts Current Anonymous Users?

    A. ICMP

    B. FTP

    C. IP

    D. TCP

    E. SNMP

4-11   Which Performance Monitor counter charts Logon Attempts?

    A. ICMP

    B. FTP

    C. IP

    D. TCP

    E. SNMP

4-12   What must be installed on a Windows NT system in order to use Performance Monitor with TCP/IP performance counters?

    A. UDP

    B. SNMP

    C. ICMP

    D. IGRP

    E. RIP

SAMPLE TEST

4-13   Which Performance Monitor counter charts Received Destination Unreachable?

    A. ICMP

    B. FTP

    C. IP

    D. TCP

    E. SNMP

4-14   Which Performance Monitor counter charts Segments/Second?

    A. ICMP

    B. FTP

    C. IP

    D. TCP

    E. UDP

4-15   Which Performance Monitor counter charts Files Sent?

    A. ICMP

    B. FTP

    C. IP

    D. TCP

    E. UDP

4-16   Which Performance Monitor counter charts Connections Active?

    A. ICMP

    B. UDP

    C. IP

    D. TCP

    E. SNMP

4-17   Which Performance Monitor counter charts Datagrams Received?

    A. ICMP

    B. FTP

    C. IP

    D. TCP

    E. SNMP

4-18   Which Performance Monitor counter charts Received Echo/Second?

    A. ICMP

    B. FTP

    C. IP

    D. TCP

    E. SNMP

4-19 You want to monitor an NT server's performance as an IP router. Which counter should you add to monitor this parameter?

    A. ICMP messages/second

    B. IP Datagrams Forwarded/second

    C. TCP Packets/second

    D. SNMP MIBs/second

    E. IGRP Routes/second

4-20 Which Performance Counter Object Type should be monitored when using PING?

    A. ICMP

    B. IP

    C. TCP

    D. SNMP

    E. UDP

4-21 Which Performance Counter Object Type should be monitored for router performance?

    A. ICMP

    B. IP

    C. TCP

    D. SNMP

    E. UDP

SAMPLE TEST

4-22 Which Performance Counter Object Type should be monitored for active connections?

    A. ICMP

    B. IP

    C. TCP

    D. SNMP

    E. UDP

4-23 Which checkbox will notify of an incorrect community name used by an SNMP manager?

    A. Only Accept SNMP Packets from These Hosts

    B. Send Authentication Trap

    C. Send Trap with Community Names

    D. Warn Administrator of Security Violations

    E. Send Alarm with Community Names

4-24 Where does an SNMP MIB reside?

    A. Agent computer only

    B. Agent and management station

    C. Management station only

    D. Network Monitor utility

    E. Caching-only agents

4-25   Where are Authentication Traps sent?

    A. Security Log in Event Viewer

    B. Messenger service

    C. Trap Destination

    D. Alerter service

    E. Warning service

4-26   What is the name of the object information database used in SNMP?

    A. MIB

    B. Trap

    C. Community name

    D. Alarm file

    E. MID

4-27   SNMP must be installed as a prerequisite to using some parts of

_____.

    A. UDP

    B. TCP/IP

    C. Performance Monitor

    D. Network Client Administrator

    E. ICMP

4-28 When configuring a Windows NT system, which is also acting as an IP router, what SNMP Agent service should be checked?

    A. Physical

    B. Datalink/Subnetwork

    C. Internet

    D. End-to-End

    E. Applications

4-29 What information on both the management application and the SNMP agent must be configured identically?

    A. Trap destination

    B. Community name

    C. IP address

    D. UDP address

    E. ARP cache

4-30 You're using SNMPMon to monitor an SNMP agent and log its data into a database. The table into which you want to log the data is called CLIENTS, but you mistype it as CLIENT. What will happen to the logged data?

    A. The data will not be logged.

    B. The data will be logged into the table with the name closest to the one you supplied (that is, CLIENTS).

    C. The data will be logged into a new table named CLIENT.

    D. None of the above.

4-31 Which of the following is/are valid SNMP monitoring conditions? Choose all that apply.

    A. NO_RESPSONSE

    B. UNSUPPORTED

    C. /=x

    D. SUPPORTED

4-32 If a monitored node description contains more than one conditional, how is it determined which conditions are logged?

    A. All are logged, in the order in which they appear.

    B. All are logged, in the order in which they're met.

    C. Only the first one met is logged.

    D. All value conditionals are logged, but only one response conditional is logged.

4-33 The total number of connections made to the `ftp` service since it was started, counting only those in which the user was able to log on to the service, can be recorded with which of the following `ftp` counters?

    A. Logon Attempts

    B. Connection Attempts

    C. Current Connections

    D. Maximum Connections

4-34   How do you install Network Monitor?

A. Choose Control Panel ➤ Network ➤ Protocols.

B. Choose Control Panel ➤ Network ➤ Bindings.

C. Choose Control Panel ➤ Network ➤ Services.

D. Requires Windows NT Server 4.0 Resource Kit.

E. Type **setup /z**.

4-35   Which of the following cannot be determined with the Network Monitor? Choose all that apply.

A. Address of sender

B. TCP packets sent during a given interval

C. Proportion of broadcast messages to directed messages within a given interval

D. None of the above

U N I T

5

Troubleshooting

Test Objectives: Troubleshooting

- **Diagnose and resolve IP addressing problems.**

- **Use Microsoft TCP/IP utilities to diagnose IP configuration problems.**

  – Identify which Microsoft TCP/IP utility to use to diagnose IP configuration problems.

- **Diagnose and resolve name resolution problems.**

Exam objectives are subject to change at any time without prior notice and at Microsoft's sole discretion. Please visit Microsoft's Training and Certification Web site (www.microsoft.com/Train_Cert/) for the most current listing of exam objectives.

TCP/IP's flexibility and the degree of control it gives the user can be an advantage, but botched configurations can lead to communications problems. Read on to learn more about probable causes of IP-addressing and name-resolution problems and about the tools Microsoft supplies with Windows NT to help you resolve them.

IP-Addressing Problems

IP-addressing problems can be the result of any of the following:

- More than one computer is attempting to use the same address.
- The address is incorrect.
- No addresses are available.

Multiple computers can attempt to access the same address when:

- A user assigns himself an IP address that conflicts with the IP address of someone else.
- A DHCP server offers an IP address for lease when that address has been statically mapped to another machine.
- Two DHCP servers offer leases from the same pool.

An incorrect IP address can also stem from user configuration errors:

- A user assigns herself an IP address that isn't mapped to her name.
- A user supplies the wrong subnet mask in the TCP/IP Properties dialog box.

If you're using DHCP and the DHCP server goes down and takes with it all address leases, then no IP addresses are available. This is one reason to use more than one DHCP server.

Using TCP/IP Utilities to Resolve IP-Configuration Problems

Those are the problems, and the resolutions seem clear:

- Fix the conflict.
- Use the proper IP address.
- Ensure that addresses are available for lease.

But how can you diagnose the problems in the first place? Windows NT Server comes with several command-line utilities that display configuration information which helps you resolve TCP/IP problems (see Table 5.1).

T A B L E 5.1 TCP/IP diagnostic utilities	**Utility**	**Description**
	arp	Displays and modifies the tables used by the Address Resolution Protocol to map IP addresses to physical addresses.
	hostname	Prints the name of the host on which the command is issued. Has no further parameters.
	ipconfig	Displays current TCP/IP configuration values, including IP address, subnet mask, and default gateway.
	nbtstat	Displays protocol statistics and current TCP/IP connections for computers running NetBIOS over TCP/IP (NBT).
	netstat	Displays protocol statistics and current TCP/IP connections for TCP/IP hosts.
	ping	Verifies connections to computers, using either names or IP addresses.
	route*	Displays and manipulates route tables.
	tracert	Determines the route packets take to a destination.

*Covered in Unit 2

arp

When you send a packet across a TCP/IP network, name resolution is only half the battle when it comes to getting the packet to its destination. The IP address must also be mapped to a hardware address for packet delivery. The utility in charge of doing this mapping is arp, which creates a cache of IP address-to-network address mappings and then refers to it each time a packet is sent so as to attach the physical address.

To track down duplicate IP addresses assigned to more than one physical address, you can view and edit the contents of the arp cache with the arp command, which uses the following syntax (see Table 5.2):

```
arp -a [inet_addr] [-N [if_addr]]
arp -d inet_addr [if_addr]
arp -s inet_addr ether_addr [if_addr]
```

T A B L E 5.2 arp parameters	Parameter	Function
	-a or -g	Displays the current contents of the arp cache.
	-d	Deletes the entry specified by inet_addr.
	-s	Adds a static entry to the cache, mapping an IP address to a physical address.
	-N	Displays the arp entries for the specified physical address.
	inet_addr	Specifies an IP address, written in dotted decimal format.
	if_addr	Specifies, if present, the IP address of the NIC whose cache should be modified. If it has no IP address, the first NIC is used.
	ether_addr	Specifies a physical address (for either Ethernet or Token Ring cards) written as six hexadecimal bytes separated by hyphens.

Normal arp cache entries are dynamic and removed after a given time interval. Entries added are static but not persistent across system boots.

ipconfig

The ipconfig utility displays IP-addressing information for the local network adapter or one specified by name.

To get the name of an adapter, type **ipconfig** without parameters. This command displays the network adapter's name, IP address, default gateway, and subnet mask.

The command's syntax is as follows:

```
ipconfig [/all | /renew [adapter] | /release [adapter]]
```

Below is a list of the parameters:

- /all displays all information about all local adapters, including:
  - Network adapter's name, IP address, default gateway, subnet mask, physical address (in hexadecimal), and a short physical description
  - The host name (computer name)
  - The name of any DNS servers
  - The node type
  - The scope ID being used
  - Whether IP routing is enabled for this machine
  - Whether a WINS proxy is in use
  - Whether NetBIOS name resolution uses DNS (refers to DNS first so that DNS can refer to WINS)
- /renew renews the lease for the specified adapter or for all local adapters if none is named.

- /release releases the DHCP lease for the specified adapter (or for all local adapters if none is named) and thus disables TCP/IP for this adapter.

- adapter is the name of the adapter.

The renew and release commands are available only on DHCP clients.

nbtstat

Resolution of NetBIOS names over TCP/IP is done with NetBT. This function is used for WINS and DNS name resolution, local cache lookup, and referral to LMHOSTS and HOSTS files. To troubleshoot name-to-address mappings, you can use nbtstat, which uses the following syntax (see Table 5.3):

```
nbtstat [-a remotename] [-A IPaddress] [-c] [-n] [-R] [-r]
[-S] [-s] [interval]
```

	Parameter	Function
T A B L E 5.3 nbtstat parameters	-a remotename	Lists the remote computer's name table by the remote computer's name.
	-A IPaddress	Lists the remote computer's name table by the remote computer's IP address.
	-c	Lists the contents of the name cache, mapping each IP address to a name.
	-n	Lists local NetBIOS names.
	-R	If LMHOSTS Lookup is enabled (in the TCP/IP Properties dialog box), reloads the name cache after purging its current contents.

T A B L E 5.3 *(cont.)*	Parameter	Function
nbtstat parameters	-r	Lists name-resolution statistics for Windows networking. On computers connected to a WINS server, this command displays the names resolved with WINS and those resolved with broadcasts.
	-S	Displays workstation and server sessions, listing hosts by IP address.
	-s	Displays workstation and server sessions, attempting to list hosts by name.
	interval	The number of seconds between refreshes of statistics.

netstat

Use this command to display protocol statistics and get information about TCP/IP connections. Its syntax is as follows (see Table 5.4):

```
netstat [-a] [-e][-n][-s] [-p protocol] [-r] [interval]
```

T A B L E 5.4	Parameter	Description
netstat parameters	-a	Displays connections and listening ports and their current state, but not server sessions.
	-e	Displays Ethernet statistics.
	-n	Displays active connections, listed by IP address.
	-s	Displays per-protocol statistics for IP, ICMP, TCP, and UDP.
	-p protocol	Displays active connection statistics for the chosen protocol (TCP or UDP). If used with the -s switch, may display statistics for TCP, UDP, IP, or ICMP.
	-r	Displays the contents of the routing table.
	interval	The number of seconds between refreshes of statistics.

ping

The ping utility sends ICMP echo packets to verify connections to a remote host (or, if used with the loopback address, to check the local connection to the network). Its syntax (see Table 5.5) is as follows:

```
ping [-t] [-a] [-n count] [-l length] [-f] [-i ttl] [-v tos]
[-r count] [-s count] [[-j host-list] | [-k host-list]] [-w
timeout] destination-list
```

TABLE 5.5	Parameter	Description
ping parameters	-t	Pings the specified host until interrupted.
	-a	Pings the specified address and resolves it to a host name.
	-n count	Sends the number of echo packets specified by count (by default, 4).
	-l length	Sends echo packets of the size specified with length. The default is 64 bytes; the maximum is 8192.
	-f	Sends a Do Not Fragment command in the packet's flags so that gateways don't fragment the echo packet.
	-i ttl	Sets the time to live field with the value specified in ttl. Time to live is the measure of how many hops a datagram can take before timing out; each time the datagram hops to a new router, its ttl is decremented by 1. If a datagram's ttl reaches 0 before its destination then the transmission will time out.
	-v tos	Sets the type of service field to that with the value of tos.
	-r count	Records the route of the outgoing and returning packets for count hops. count can be a value in the range 1 to 9.
	-s count	Specifies the timestamp for the number of hosts specified by count.
	-j host-list	Routes packets via the list of hosts (up to 9) specified in host-list. The route may include intermediate gateways.

T A B L E 5.5 (cont.) ping parameters	Parameter	Description
	`-k host-list`	Routes packets via the list of hosts (up to 9) specified in `host-list`. The route may not include intermediate gateways.
	`-w timeout`	Specifies the timeout (in milliseconds) to wait for each reply before reporting a failure. You can specify as much as one second.
	`destination-list`	Specifies the remote hosts to `ping`, by domain name or by IP address.

You can use `ping` to test name resolution. If you can ping a host by IP address but not by name, be sure that a name mapping is in the HOSTS file or in DNS.

tracert

You use the `tracert` utility to determine the route a packet took to reach its destination. This utility sends ICMO echo packets with varying TTL values that are decremented each time a packet hops to a new subnet. Essentially, tracert sends the first packet with a TTL of 1 and then keeps incrementing further packet TTL counts by 1 until the target responds or until the maximum TTL is reached. The command syntax (see Table 5.6) is as follows:

```
tracert [-d] [-h maximum_hops] [-j host-list] [-w timeout]
target_name
```

T A B L E 5.6 tracert parameters	Parameter	Description
	`-d`	Specifies that IP addresses should not be resolved to the host name.
	`-h maximum hops`	Specifies the maximum number of hops that can be used to search for the target.

T A B L E 5.6 *(cont.)* tracert parameters	Parameter	Description
	`-j host-list`	Specifies a loose source route (that is, that the route should follow a certain path but that intermediate gateways can be involved).
	`-w timeout`	Waits the number of milliseconds specified by `timeout` for each reply.
	`target_name`	Specifies the name of the target host.

Name-Resolution Problems

If you can't connect to a resource or ping it, first check for a name resolution problem. Try pinging the resource by IP address. If you can reach it, the problem lies not with the connection but with the entry in the HOSTS or LMHOSTS file or with your access to it.

First, be sure you can get to the database of name-to-address mappings:

- If the copy of HOSTS or LMHOSTS is stored locally, be sure that it's present and in the proper location.

- If you're using DNS or WINS for name resolution, ping the servers.

- If you can't reach the server(s), ensure that you've got the right IP address for them in your computer's TCP/IP properties and that the servers are up. Ping another computer on the same segment as the name resolution server to be sure that the problem is with the server and not with that portion of the network.

If you can get to the servers, check their name-resolution databases, and check the Services applet in Control Panel to be sure that any name-resolution services are running.

DNS servers refer to HOSTS files; WINS servers may refer to LMHOSTS files in addition to their databases.

You won't be able to resolve a name in a HOSTS file if:

- No entry exists for that name-address mapping.

- The host name is misspelled or uses different capitalization (host names are case-sensitive).

- The IP address is incorrect.

- The HOSTS file contains multiple addresses for the same host but on different lines.

- It's really an LMHOSTS entry mistakenly added to the wrong file.

Using DNS and DHCP in combination can easily lead to name-resolution problems, because no mechanism exists to automatically update the DNS database. Hosts in the DNS database should have static name-address mappings. Use addresses excluded from DHCP's lease pool or permanent leases.

You won't be able to resolve a name in an LMHOSTS file if:

- No entry exists for the name.

- The name in the file is spelled differently from the way you spelled it when attempting to connect. (LMHOSTS entries are not case-sensitive.)

- The IP address is incorrect.

IP-Addressing Problems

1. How does TTL limit the number of routers a datagram may traverse?

_____

_____

2. True or False: If arp does not find the destination host MAC address on its subnet, it will forward the query through the router to the destination's subnet for resolution.

3. How can having two DHCP servers lead to addressing problems?

_____

_____

4. To ensure that statically mapped addresses are not leased, they should be

_____.

5. All users in your network are using fixed IP addresses. People trying to connect to John's machine are unable to do so. You've checked, and he's using the correct IP address, and it's not conflicting with anyone else's. What else could be wrong with John's local configuration?

_____

_____

6. True or False: To avoid IP addressing problems, it's a good idea to have only a single DHCP server.

Using TCP/IP Utilities to Resolve IP Configuration Problems

7. To find the path that data packets will take to reach a destination, use

_____.

8. What problem does a "gratuitous" ARP Request detect?

_____

9. _____ is responsible for mapping hardware to IP

addresses.

10. What command is most useful to verify TCP/IP configuration information?

_____

11. What command should be used to reload the NetBIOS name cache?

_____

12. What does TTL stand for?

_____

13. The _____ -c command may be executed on an NT system to view the NetBIOS
Remote Cache Name Table.

14. What command is most helpful in verifying basic IP connectivity?

_____

15. What is the most common use of the Do Not Fragment option of the ping command?

_____

16. The _____ file provides network name to network IP address resolution.

17. What command is used on a Windows NT Server to detect invalid physical address entries in the local computer's cache?

_____

18. True or False: If you add a static entry to the arp cache, this entry will not be affected by time interval and will remain persistent across reboots.

19. The ipconfig parameters /release and /renew are available only on a _____ client.

20. The netstat - p command (with no other parameters) will permit you to view statistics for the _____ and _____ protocols.

21. The tracert utility uses _____ echo packets.

Name Resolution Problems

22. How does an h-node resolve NetBIOS names when a WINS server is not responding?

_____

23. True or False: A system configured to use broadcasting for NetBIOS name resolution could also be configured to use the LMHOSTS file to communicate with remote hosts across a router in a non-WINS environment.

24. A user can reach the Unix host via ftp on an NT system using the Unix host's IP address, but an attempt to reach the host using the Unix hostname fails. What file name on the NT system should be checked?

_____

25. True or False: If a NetBIOS client receives a response from a primary WINS server that it does not have a name/address mapping for the client's request, the client will proceed to check the secondary WINS server for resolution.

26. Provide two examples of how you could use ping to detect and resolve name-resolution problems.

_____

_____

_____

_____

27. True or False: Entries in a HOSTS file are case-sensitive.

28. How can using DNS and DHCP together lead to name-resolution problems?

_____

_____

29. You can't resolve a fully qualified domain name that should have an entry in the centralized database. Which name resolution service is involved?

_____

S A M P L E   T E S T

5-1 How do you verify that WINS services are running?

    A. From the command line, type **WINS /?**.

    B. Choose Control Panel ➤ Services.

    C. Choose Control Panel ➤ Network ➤ WINS Configuration.

    D. Choose Control Panel ➤ WINS ➤ WINS Services.

    E. Choose Control Panel ➤ WINS ➤ WINS Startup.

5-2 What command will restart a WINS server that is stopped?

    A. `WINS Start`

    B. `Start WINS`

    C. `Net Start WINS`

    D. `winsvcs /start`

    E. `winstart`

5-3 Which network address from the route table must never appear on any network?

    A. 127.0.0.0

    B. 0.0.0.0

    C. 255.255.255.255

    D. 1.2.3.4

    E. 124.125.126.127

SAMPLE TEST

5-4 When a `ping` is generated for a remote host on a distant subnet, the requesting host's `arp` cache is consulted for:

   A. The remote host's hardware address

   B. The default gateway's hardware address

   C. The local host's IP address

   D. The remote host's IP address

   E. The remote host's default gateway address

5-5 TTL is measured in:

   A. Hop count through routers

   B. Seconds

   C. Milliseconds

   D. Quarter-seconds

5-6 Which byte is appended to the end of the COMPUTERNAME to form the NetBIOS Workstation service name?

   A. 00h

   B. 01h

   C. 03h

   D. 20h

   E. 23h

SAMPLE TEST

5-7   Which byte is appended to the end of the COMPUTERNAME to form the NetBIOS Messenger service name?

    A. 00h

    B. 01h

    C. 03h

    D. 20h

    E. 23h

5-8   Which byte is appended to the end of the COMPUTERNAME to form the NetBIOS Server service name?

    A. 00h

    B. 01h

    C. 03h

    D. 20h

    E. 23h

5-9   Receiving the Destination Host Unreachable message from the `ping` command means that:

    A. The remote host may be powered off or that TCP/IP is disabled.

    B. The default gateway to the remote host is probably down.

    C. The route table has no route entry for the destination host.

    D. `ping` has timed out and assumes that the host is currently unreachable.

    E. `arp` has failed to find the local gateway's physical address.

UNIT

6

Final Review

FINAL REVIEW

You've studied the material and taken the unit exams. Now, let's see how you do on a representation of the real thing. The number of questions and the time associated with each question on each Microsoft certification exam varies, but the ratio of time to questions is fairly consistent—you'll have about a minute and a half to two minutes for each question.

All set? Then let's go. Good luck!

1   DNS was originally designed to replace the _____ file.

    A. LMHOSTS

    B. NAMES

    C. DOMAINS

    D. HOSTS

    E. SERVICES

2   You're running an IIS server offering data transfer services, and you want to find out how many people who don't require a personal user account are using the service. Which Performance Monitor object would you watch?

    A. ICMP

    B. FTP

    C. IP

    D. TCP

    E. SNMP

3 Which of the following is/are a valid host address on a Class B network? Choose all that apply.

    A. 116.48.17.52

    B. 190.64.90.2

    C. 148.200.87.0

    D. 240.78.99.15

4 Choose a phrase to complete the following sentence. Use of WINS _____ Microsoft clients.

    A. Increases the number of IP broadcasts generated by

    B. Decreases the number of IP broadcasts generated by

    C. Does not affect the number of IP broadcasts generated by

    D. Decreases the number of ARP requests generated by

    E. Increases the number of ARP requests generated by

5 You're maintaining a secure server that requires a user account to log on. If you wanted to know how many people were logged on to IIS at a given time to download files, which of the following counters would you use? Choose all that apply.

    A. Current Connections

    B. Logon Attempts

    C. Maximum Nonanonymous Users

    D. Current Nonanonymous Users

6   You have a large LAN you want to segment with a 6-port bridge. Assuming a Class C address, which of the following subnet masks should you use? Choose all that apply.

    A. 255.255.255.0

    B. 255.255.255.224

    C. 255.255.255.248

    D. 255.255.248.0

    E. None of the above

7   The DNS PTR record for the IP address 154.94.37.25 is:

    A. 154.94.37.25.inaddr.arpa

    B. in-addr.arpa.154.94.37.25

    C. 25.37.94.154.in-add-arpA.

    D. 25.37.94.154.in-addr.arpa

    E. inaddr-arpA.255.255.255.255

8   A _____ DNS query is made when the client requests the host name by giving the host's IP address.

    A. Name

    B. Recursive

    C. Iterative

    D. Reverse

    E. Forward

9   A DNS server designated to communicate with a network external to the corporation is called a(n) _____.

    A. Iterative server

    B. DNS relay server

    C. Gateway

    D. Firewall

    E. Forwarder

10   Which of the following does `ftp` use? Choose all that apply.

    A. UDP

    B. TCP

    C. ICMP

    D. IP

    E. SNMP

11   You have a slash-26 network with a subnet mask of 255.255.255.192. A Windows NT Server domain controller on the network has an address of 195.50.30.70. Which of the following would be a valid address for a Windows 95 client on the network?

    A. 195.50.30.0

    B. 195.50.30.196

    C. 195.50.30.198

    D. 195.50.30.256

    E. 195.50.30.70

12   What dynamic routing protocol does Windows NT 4 use to update its routing tables?

    A. OSPF

    B. MPR

    C. DRP

    D. RIP

    E. UDP

13   Microsoft's implementation of NBNS under RFC 1001/1002 is called:

    A. DHCP

    B. WINS

    C. DNS

    D. MPR

    E. RIP

14   The total number of connections made to the ftp service since it was started, counting only those in which the user was able to log on to the service, can be recorded with which of the following ftp counters?

    A. Logon Attempts

    B. Connection Attempts

    C. Current Connections

    D. Maximum Connections

15   How many scopes should be created within DHCP for a single subnet?

    A. 5

    B. 1

    C. An unlimited number, but you need to use the Registry Editor

    D. 2

    E. 10

16   Server A is a primary WINS server, and Server B is the secondary WINS server. Choose a replication strategy from the following list:

    A. A is push partner, B is pull partner.

    B. A is push and pull partner, B is pull partner.

    C. A and B are push and pull partners.

    D. A is pull partner, B is push partner.

    E. A and B are replication partners by default.

17   A WINS push partner updates its pull partner by:

    A. Sending the entire WINS database to it

    B. Notifying the pull partner that it has updates

    C. Sending changes only without notification

    D. Requesting its version number

    E. Merging updates with the database

18   Which DHCP option type should be changed to configure the default gateway for multiple networks?

    A. Global

    B. Scope

    C. Default

    D. Router

    E. Gateway

19   Which of the following is/are benefits of DHCP? Choose all that apply.

    A. No need for user TCP/IP configuration

    B. No need to register the host name

    C. No need to reconfigure stations that change subnets

    D. No need for administrator to perform IP subnet calculations

    E. No need for HOSTS files

20   You have noticed a high number of Datagrams Outbound Discarded in Performance Monitor. Of what is this a symptom?

    A. Invalid default gateway

    B. Invalid subnet mask

    C. Lack of buffer space

    D. Invalid physical address

    E. Invalid ARP cache

21   Your internetwork has two DHCP servers for redundancy purposes, one on each of two subnets. To ensure that a pool of IP addresses is available for each subnet even if one of the servers goes down, how should you configure the two servers?

    A. Each with 50% different IP address scopes

    B. Each with 100% same IP address scopes

    C. One with 75%, the other with the remaining 25%

    D. Each with 100% different IP address scopes

    E. Each with alternating IP address scopes

22   From which of the following protocols is DHCP derived?

    A. ICMP

    B. UDP

    C. SNMP

    D. BOOTP

    E. TCP

23   Which of the following may be a DHCP server? Choose all that apply.

    A. Windows for Workgroup 3.11

    B. Windows NT Workstation 3.51

    C. Windows NT Server 4

    D. Windows 95

    E. Windows NT Workstation 4

24   Which checkbox will notify of an invalid community name used by an SNMP manager?

    A. Only Accept SNMP Packets from These Hosts

    B. Send Authentication Trap

    C. Send Trap with Community Names

    D. Warn Administrator of Security Violations

    E. Send Alarm with Community Names

25   What does RIP use for a transport protocol?

    A. ARP

    B. TCP

    C. UDP

    D. IP

    E. ICMP

26   What is `telnet` used for?

    A. File transfer

    B. Terminal emulation

    C. Browsing

    D. Printing

    E. Troubleshooting

27   Which of the following is a valid IP address on a network with an IP address of 10.192.0.0 and a subnet mask of 255.255.0.0? Choose all that apply.

    A. 10.192.26.0

    B. 10.192.26.255

    C. 10.192.27.0

    D. 10.193.26.0

28   What print destination is used for TCP/IP printing to a Unix-host printer?

    A. Digital Network port

    B. Local port

    C. LPR port

    D. Other...

    E. LPQ port

29   Which of the following is not set in the SNMP Properties dialog box? Choose all that apply.

    A. The contact name

    B. The contact e-mail address

    C. The types of services for which SNMP will be used

    D. The computers from which SNMP is capable of receiving packets

30   LMHOSTS entries with the #PRE directive should be:

    A. Placed at the beginning of the file for faster loading into the cache

    B. Placed at the end of the file, as they will not be accessed after TCP initializes

    C. Placed anywhere in the file, as they are comments only

    D. Left out of the LMHOSTS file, as #PRE only applies to the HOSTS file

    E. Placed at the end, except when used with the #DOM directive

31   A DNS zone transfer:

    A. Copies only the changes from the primary to the secondary

    B. Copies the entire database from the primary to the secondary

    C. Copies the updates entered in the DNSUPD.LOG file from the primary to the secondary

    D. Copies the DNS cache from the primary to the secondary

    E. Copies the DNS cache from the secondary to the cache-only server

32   You want to find out the rate at which datagrams are discarded for reasons other than errors. Which Performance Monitor object would you be looking at?

    A. ICMP

    B. FTP

    C. IP

    D. TCP

    E. UDP

33 Which of the following is a requirement for a Microsoft client to print to a TCP/IP-enabled printer?

    A. Client must have NetBIOS enabled.

    B. Client must have printer defined in HOSTS or LMHOSTS.

    C. Windows NT system with TCP/IP printing must be installed.

    D. Windows NT system must have DNS enabled with printer defined in PRINTCAP file.

    E. Windows NT with SNMP installed.

34 The LPD service must be supported by the Unix host if a Windows NT system is to:

    A. Run commands remotely on the host

    B. Send print jobs to the host

    C. Copy files between the Windows NT Server and the host

    D. Receive print jobs from the host

35 A previously configured DHCP client that later reboots will send a
_____ message to the DHCP server during its IP configuration.

    A. Dhcpdiscover

    B. Dhcpoffer

    C. Dhcprequest

    D. Dhcpack

    E. Dhcpnak

36   If you do not specify a server when using the rsh command, what will happen?

   A. The command will not work.

   B. The command will execute on the local host.

   C. The command will execute on the host to which the user is currently logged on.

   D. None of the above.

37   The DHCP server on your company's network has a scope containing IP addresses ranging from 197.45.3.27 to 197.45.3.42, excluding addresses 197.45.3.35 to 197.45.3.41. The addresses that your network has range from 197.45.3.0 to 197.45.3.50. If you disable DHCP support in your RAS settings for TCP/IP, what is the largest contiguous block of addresses you could specify to be allocated to RAS clients?

   A. 50

   B. 27

   C. 26

   D. None of the above

38   Which of the following protocol combinations does SNMP use for transport?

   A. WINSOCK over IP

   B. UDP over IP

   C. TCP over IP

   D. TCP over ICMP

   E. UDP over ICMP

39 What's the cause of fragmentation failures?

   A. Disks that are too full.

   B. Transmission failures with ping or ftp.

   C. A datagram has its Do Not Fragment bit set, but the MTU of a router it's passing through is too small for the datagram.

   D. IP traffic is too heavy on the network to transmit data properly.

40 You want to monitor datagrams forwarded in Performance Monitor to evaluate an NT system's overall performance as an IP router. Which of the following protocols must you install? Choose all that apply.

   A. SMTP

   B. AARP

   C. SNMP

   D. ARP

   E. UDP

41 Which Performance Monitor object charts the number of connections established?

   A. ICMP

   B. FTP

   C. IP

   D. TCP

   E. SNMP

42   Which `ftp` command will suppress prompting during multiple file transfers?

    A. `ftp -s`

    B. `ftp -i`

    C. `ftp -d`

    D. `ftp -v`

    E. `ftp /s`

43   You want to see the rate at which sent packets are bouncing because the destination is inaccessible from your server. Which Performance Monitor object should you use?

    A. ICMP

    B. FTP

    C. IP

    D. TCP

    E. SNMP

44   Which Performance Monitor object has counters that can chart the rate at which a computer receives `ping` attempts?

    A. ICMP

    B. FTP

    C. IP

    D. TCP

    E. SNMP

45   You want to monitor an NT server's performance as an IP router. Which counter should you add to monitor this parameter?

    A. ICMP Messages/second

    B. IP Datagrams Forwarded/second

    C. TCP Packets/second

    D. SNMP MIBs/second

    E. IGRP Routes/second

46   Which command will restart the WINS service if it's stopped?

    A. WINS Start

    B. Start WINS

    C. Net Start WINS

    D. winsvcs /start

    E. winstart

47   Where does an SNMP MIB reside?

    A. Agent computer only

    B. Agent and management station

    C. Management station only

    D. Network Monitor utility

    E. Caching-only agents

48 To what location are authentication traps sent?

  A. Security Log in Event Viewer

  B. Messenger service

  C. Trap destination

  D. Alerter service

  E. Warning service

49 SNMP must be installed as a prerequisite to using some parts of

_____.

  A. UDP

  B. TCP/IP

  C. Performance Monitor

  D. Network Client Administrator

  E. ICMP

50 Which of the following must be the same on both the management application and the SNMP agent?

  A. Trap destination

  B. Community name

  C. IP address

  D. UDP address

  E. ARP cache

51   How do you verify that WINS services are running?

  A. At the command line, type **WINS /?**.

  B. Choose Control Panel ➤ Services.

  C. Choose Control Panel ➤ Network ➤ WINS Configuration.

  D. Choose Control Panel ➤ WINS ➤ WINS Services.

  E. Choose Control Panel ➤ WINS ➤ WINS Startup.

52   You have a large LAN you want to segment with a 6-port router. Assuming a Class C address, what mask should you use?

  A. 255.255.255.0

  B. 255.255.255.224

  C. 255.255.255.248

  D. 255.255.255.192

  E. 255.255.224.0

53   Which `ftp` command will automatically execute commands from a file?

  A. `ftp -s: filename host`

  B. `ftp -f: filename host`

  C. `ftp filename host | scriptfile`

  D. `ftp filename host > scriptfile`

  E. `ftp /filename`

54   What domain is configured by option 15 in DHCP?

    A. Windows NT domain

    B. DNS domain

    C. NIS domain

    D. Default domain

    E. Eminent domain

55   Which of the following must be installed on a Windows NT system in order to use Performance Monitor with TCP/IP performance counters?

    A. UDP

    B. SNMP

    C. ICMP

    D. IGRP

    E. RIP

56   What two pieces of information do you need to create a Windows NT print queue for a Unix printer?

    A. Reserved address in DHCP scope

    B. The IP address or host name of the host to which the printer is connected

    C. Static mapping or LMHOST entry in WINS-enabled networks

    D. Printer name as identified on the host

    E. Printer name in HOSTS file

57   If you want to keep track of what's going on with `ping`, which Performance Monitor object should you track?

    A. ICMP

    B. IP

    C. TCP

    D. SNMP

    E. UDP

58   Which of the following *must* be entered to configure a DHCP server?

    A. DNS address

    B. IP address

    C. Primary WINS server

    D. Scope ID

    E. Subnet mask

59   Which of the following can be managed with SNMP?

    A. WINS

    B. IIS

    C. DNS

    D. DHCP

60   Which of the following utilities use ICMP as their base protocol? Choose all that apply.

    A. ftp

    B. tracert

    C. tftp

    D. ping

61   You're using SNMPMon to monitor an SNMP agent and log its data into a database. The table in the database into which you want to log the data is called NORMAL, but you mistype it as NORMLA. What will happen to the logged data?

    A. The data will not be logged.

    B. The data will be logged into the table with the name closest to the one you supplied (that is, NORMAL).

    C. The data will be logged into a new table named NORMLA.

    D. None of the above.

62   Which of the following is/are valid SNMP monitoring conditions? Choose all that apply.

    A. NO_RESPSONSE

    B. UNSUPPORTED

    C. <x

    D. RESPONDED

FINAL REVIEW

63   Which of the following cannot be determined with the Network Monitor? Choose all that apply.

    A. Address of sender

    B. TCP packets sent during a given interval

    C. Proportion of broadcast messages to directed messages within a given interval

    D. None of the above

64   If a monitored node description contains more than one conditional, which one(s) will be logged if logging is enabled?

    A. All are logged, in the order in which they appear.

    B. All are logged, in the order in which they're met.

    C. Only the first one met is logged.

    D. All value conditionals are logged, but only one response conditional is logged.

65   You're trying to set up an SNMP monitoring configuration file to record how often toast is burned by monitoring the object toastDoneness. Assuming that properly done toast falls within a range of 3–7 in a range of 1–10, which of the following in a conditional statement would log the event whenever toast is burned?

    A. =8

    B. >7

    C. /=3-7

    D. None of the above

FINAL REVIEW

66   You have a Class B network with 6 subnets. The 200 laptop clients frequently roam between these subnets. Which of the following options will allocate IP addresses most effectively?

    A. Central DHCP and DNS server with long lease time.

    B. DHCP server on each subnet with short lease time.

    C. DHCP server on each subnet with default lease time.

    D. DHCP and WINS server on each subnet with long lease time.

    E. You have too many clients for this network.

67   How do you install Network Monitor?

    A. Choose Control Panel ➤ Network ➤ Protocols.

    B. Choose Control Panel ➤ Network ➤ Services.

    C. Choose Control Panel ➤ Network ➤ Bindings.

    D. From the Windows NT Server 4.0 Resource Kit.

    E. Type **setup /z**.

68   Which tool would you use first to help you determine what went wrong when a TCP/IP service failed to start?

    A. The Performance Monitor

    B. The Network Monitor

    C. The SNMP Service

    D. The Event Viewer

APPENDIX

Study Questions and
Sample Test Answers

Unit 1 Answers

Study Questions

1. 255.255.252.0

   Explanation: This is a Class B IP address. The subnet mask 255.255.252.0 produces 62 subnets with 1022 hosts. Other combinations yield fewer hosts or do not yield the minimum required subnets.

2. 30

   Explanation: This is a Class C network. A subnet mask of 255.255.255.224 yields a network with 6 subnets and 30 hosts. 224 = 11100000 (binary). Three bits are set to 1, used for the subnet, and 5 bits are set to zero, available for host assignment. 2 to the 3rd power equals 8 ($2^3=8$), minus 2 reserved addresses equals 6 subnets available. On the host side, $2^5=32$, minus 2 reserved addresses equals 30 hosts per subnet.

3. 254

   Explanation: This is a Class C IP address. The default subnet mask of 255.255.255.0 allows use of all 8 bits (11111111 binary) for host addressing. This yields 2 to the 8th power=256 host addresses, but 2 are reserved. 256-2=254.

4. 62

   Explanation: This is a Class C IP address. A subnet mask of 255.255.255.252 yields 62 subnets with 2 hosts per subnet. Other subnet masks yield fewer subnets.

5. 255.255.255.0

   Explanation: These are Class B addresses in the range 128 to 191. Class B addresses use the first two octets for the network portion of the IP address by default. Since the third octet is the same in both addresses, it must be subnetted.

6. 255.255.255.240

Explanation: This is a Class C IP address in the range 192 to 223. The subnet mask of 255.255.255.240 produces 14 subnets with 14 hosts per subnet. Other combinations produce fewer subnets or fewer than 10 hosts per subnet.

7. 1022

Explanation: This is a Class B IP address subnetted with 62 subnets and 1022 hosts per subnet. The default mask is 255.255.0.0 for Class B. The given mask of 255.255.252.0 gives 6 bits in the third octet (252 = 11111100) for the network ID and 2 bits for host assignment. The fourth octet is left with all 8 bits for host assignment. 8+2=10 total bits for hosts. 2 to the 10th power is 1024, minus 2 reserved addresses gives 1022 hosts.

8. 255.255.248.0

Explanation: The third octet (248) is 11111000 in binary. Five ones yield 32 possible subnets (2 to the 5th power is 32). Two subnets are always unusable for addressing—one is the base subnet, and one is used for broadcasting on the subnet. Subtracting these two unusable addresses gives 32-2=30 usable subnets.

9. 192.192.191.0 and 192.192.191.255

Explanation: This is a Class C address; the last octet is used for host addresses. An all zero or all 1 binary address may not be used for addressing hosts. All zero binary is also zero in decimal; all 1 in binary is 255 in decimal.

10. 62 (255.255.255.252)

Explanation: This is a Class C address. The maximum number of subnets that may be created on a Class C address is 62 subnets with 2 hosts per subnet, using 255.255.255.252 subnet mask.

11. 255.255.255.255

Explanation: The limited broadcast address is always 255.255.255.255. This address is limited to the local network segment and is not forwarded through a router (unless specifically configured to do so).

12. 193.192.34.255

Explanation: The directed broadcast address uses the network ID portion of the IP address given, and 255 for the host ID portion. This is a Class C address; the host portion is the last octet.

13. Class A

Explanation: The Class A network uses 8 bits for the network portion of the IP address and 24 bits for the host ID portion. Class B has twice as many bits for the network (16), and Class C has three times as many bits for the network (24).

14. Class C

Explanation: The Class C network uses 8 bits for the host ID portion of the IP address and 24 bits for the network portion. Class B uses 16 bits for network and host, and Class A uses 24 bits for host and 8 bits for network.

15. Multicasting

Explanation: Multicasting is used for broadcasting messages to a group of hosts, rather than to all hosts. This reduces network traffic.

16. 193.204.220.198

Explanation: The Windows for Workgroups client is 193.204.220.199, which must be on the 10BaseT Ethernet segment. The network interface of the router on that network (the Windows NT Server) is 193.204.220.198.

17. 190.4.4.1

Explanation: The Ethernet user should choose the default gateway, which is on its own subnet.

18. 190.2.2.1

Explanation: You should choose the default gateway, which is on the same subnet as the Token Ring.

19. Gateways must have at least two addresses (interfaces).

    Explanation: To connect to two networks, you must have at least two interfaces and, therefore, two IP addresses, one from each network.

20. 140.50.2.3

    Explanation: 140.50.2.3 is the IP address of the NT server network interface, which is on the same subnet as the Unix host (140.50.2.4). The subnet mask shows that Class B is being used as one large network, rather than being subnetted.

Sample Test

1-1   B

    Explanation: 224 in decimal is 11100000 in binary. The three 1s produce 8 subnets (2 to the third power is 8). Two of these are unusable—the base subnet and the broadcast. This yields 8-2=6 usable subnets. Other combinations yield more than 6 subnets and produce fewer hosts per subnet.

1-2   B

    Explanation: Hosts will normally have the same subnet mask if they are part of the same internetwork. They would naturally have different default gateways, since they are all on separate segments. The limited broadcast address is always 255.255.255.255 for all hosts. All hosts have the same loopback address, 127.0.0.1.

1-3   B, C, D

    Explanation: A is valid as it's a Class C address, and although the default gateway is normally assigned the "1" address by convention, it's not required. B is invalid because it's a Class B address. C is invalid because it ends in zero and is therefore a network number, and D is invalid because 240 is within the range of experimental IP numbers, not the Class C range.

Unit 2 Answers

Study Questions

Selecting a Service

1. DHCP (Dynamic Host Configuration Protocol)

2. WINS (Windows Internet Name Service)

3. DNS

4. NetBIOS names

5. You can't—DNS is required to resolve external domain names.

Configuring TCP/IP for Use in Multiple-Adapter Systems

6. Multihomed

7. False

   Explanation: A computer must be multihomed and connected to two subnets to *route* data from one subnet to another, but a computer with a single IP address can send data itself— a router will forward the data to the next subnet if the destination is not local.

8. 5

Configuring Scopes with DHCP Manager

9. When the number of clients is close to the number of assignable IP addresses, and when clients frequently move between subnets.

10. False

    Explanation: Manually configured options on a client are not overridden by DHCP.

11. 255.255.255.255

    Explanation: The client broadcasts for the DHCP server.

12. None

    Explanation: There is no coordination between DHCP servers.

13. When there is a large number of IP addresses relative to the number of DHCP clients

14. False

    Explanation: They must not have duplicate addresses between them.

15. MAC address of client

    Explanation: This is the physical address of the client, burned into the network adapter.

16. True

17. Its scope options should be set up.

    Explanation: This allows the administrator to fully configure DHCP before clients are allowed to lease configurations.

18. IP Address and Subnet Mask

19. False

    Explanation: Windows NT servers can be configured to support DHCP, not BOOTP.

20. False

    Explanation: DHCP clients do not send messages to the server to release its IP configuration.

21. As a reserved IP address, or as excluded from the range of available addresses.

    Explanation: This will prevent the WINS server's IP address from being given to a DHCP client.

22. False

    Explanation: Windows NT 4 supports DHCP and DHCP relay, but does not support BOOTP.

23. BOOTP

    Explanation: BOOTP is an older protocol that was enhanced to produce DHCP.

24. False

    Explanation: WINS servers must have an IP address manually specified.

Installing and Configuring WINS

25. One (Site #1)

    Explanation: The remote sites have only one push and pull replication partner: headquarters.

26. Three

    Explanation: The three remote sites all use the central site as a replication partner.

27. False

    Explanation: WINS clients retain their name mappings from boot to boot unless another client has taken over use of their name in the interim. A client can use a client name if no other client by that name exists on the network.

28. Make both push and pull replication partners to each other.

    Explanation: It is required that primary and secondary WINS servers be push/pull replication partners with each other.

29. Specifies how often a client re-registers its name (the default is 96 hours).

30. Broadcasts

Explanation: WINS clients register directly with the WINS server and do not need to broadcast.

31. Push, pull

32. 046 WINS/NBT Node Type

Explanation: When the WINS server option is set, the node type must also be set.

33. True

Explanation: The LMHOSTS file is not required in a WINS environment, although it can be used as a backup in case the WINS server goes down.

34. True

Explanation: WINS can be used across domains and therefore be useful for browsing within and between Windows NT domains.

35. Reduction of broadcast traffic. Dynamic update of name-resolution database.

Explanation: By using a direct IP address for name resolution, the need for broadcasting is reduced, and WINS clients names are automatically registered.

36. True

Explanation: The WINS client sends a message when Windows is shut down.

37. False

Explanation: WINS is dynamically updated.

Configuring Subnet Masks

38. False

Explanation: They both produce networks with 254 hosts on each.

39. False

Explanation: They both produce subnets of 14 hosts. The Class B address yields more subnets, however—4094 subnets compared with only 14 subnets on the Class C address.

40. 254

Explanation: The default subnet mask is 255.0.0.0, so 255.255.0.0 means the second octet is subnetted. 255 in decimal is 11111111 in binary. This gives eight 1s for subnets, or 2 to the 8th power, which is 256 in decimal. Two addresses are unusable, the base subnet and the broadcast. This yields 256-2, or 254 subnets.

41. False

Explanation: They both produce subnets of 30 hosts. The Class B address yields more subnets, however—2046 subnets compared with only 6 subnets on the Class C address.

42. 255.0.0.0

Explanation: This is a Class A IP address, which ranges from 1 to 126 in decimal.

43. Class B, 255.255.0.0

44. Class C, 255.255.255.0

45. 254

Explanation: This is a Class C IP address in the range 192 to 223. The last octet (8 bits) is used for host addressing. This produces 2 to the 8th power (256) possible addresses, but 2 are reserved. 256-2=254.

46. 255.255.255.224 or 255.255.255.240

Explanation: This is a Class C IP address. 255.255.255.224 produces 6 subnets with 30 hosts. The 255.255.255.240 subnet mask produces 14 subnets with 14 hosts.

47. 255.255.255.224

Explanation: This is a Class C IP address. 255.255.255.224 subnet mask produces 6 subnets with 30 hosts.

48. 255.255.224.0

Explanation: This is a Class B IP address. 255.255.224.0 subnet mask produces 6 subnets with 8190 hosts.

49. 255.255.0.0

Explanation: This is a Class B address, which uses 255.255.0.0 as its default subnet mask.

50. 255.255.0.0 (Class B)

Explanation: When the first two bits of an IP address are 10 (binary), the address class is B. The default subnet mask for a Class B IP address is 255.255.0.0

51. 255.0.0.0

Explanation: This is a Class A IP address, which uses 255.0.0.0 as its default subnet mask.

52. 140.50.30.255

Explanation: This is a Class B IP address subnetted on the third octet. The last octet is used for host addressing. All ones (11111111 binary) is the broadcast address, which is 255 in decimal.

53. Class B; 255.255.0.0

Explanation: Class B IP addresses are in the range 128 to 191. The default subnet mask for Class B addresses is 255.255.0.0.

54. 255.255.0.0

    Explanation: These are Class A IP addresses. The default Class A network uses the first octet for the network portion. Since the second octet is the same for both IP addresses, the network must be subnetted on the second octet.

55. 6

    Explanation: This is a Class C network. The subnet mask of 255.255.255.248 yields 30 subnets with 6 hosts per subnet. 248=11111000 (binary). There are 5 ones ($2\string^5=32$) or 32 subnets minus 2 reserved equals 30 available for assignment. The 3 zeros ($2\string^3=8$) give 8 host addresses minus 2 reserved equals 6 available for assignment per subnet.

56. 255.255.255.224

    Explanation: This is a Class C network. The subnet mask of 255.255.255.224 produces a network of 6 subnets and 30 hosts.

57. 65

    Explanation: 13 clients + 1 server + 12 clients + 4 servers + 17 clients + 3 servers + 11 clients + 4 router interfaces (one per segment).

Configuring a Windows NT Server IP Router

58. False

    Explanation: DHCP relay agents may be used to pass configuration requests to DHCP servers without requiring a DHCP server on every subnet.

59. False

    Explanation: DHCP Relay Agent does nothing for WINS.

60. 15

    Explanation: Hop count is decremented by at least one for every router the packet passes through.

61. Clear the Enable IP Forwarding checkbox.

62. DHCP Relay Agent on NT 4

    Explanation: DHCP Relay forwards DHCP broadcasts to the DHCP server.

Installing and Configuring DNS

63. Query other DNS servers and cache the results.

    Explanation: The caching-only server will not get a preload or update from other servers, but will only update itself on those specific hosts which queries have come to it first.

64. `cache.dns` on a Windows NT Server or `named.cache` on other DNS servers

    Explanation: The root-level domain name servers are placed in the `cache.dns` file on a Windows NT server. .

65. True

    Explanation: This allows the host name to be used with several different domains in an attempt to resolve the IP address.

66. False

    Explanation: The DNS name server must be specified in the TCP/IP configuration, but does not need to appear in the HOSTS file.

67. Zone transfer

    Explanation: Zone transfers update the information between the primary and secondary DNS servers.

68. Primary DNS Server via zone transfer

    Explanation: The secondary DNS server updates its DNS information from the primary. This update is called a zone transfer.

69. Does not generate zone transfer network traffic

Explanation: A caching-only server will receive requests for resolution and query other name servers. It does not receive zone-transfers and so does not generate network traffic.

70. False

Explanation: A recursive query means the DNS server queried cannot refer the client to another DNS server. It must resolve the query, report an error, or query another server. An iterative query, by contrast, means the DNS server could refer the client to another DNS server and force the client to make another DNS query against that server.

71. False

Explanation: DNS can query the WINS database to find host names, but is not itself involved in NetBIOS name resolution.

72. True

Explanation: When a Windows NT Server that is configured to forward DNS queries to WINS servers receives a query that is not in its DNS database, it forwards the query to a WINS server.

73. So that the Pointer (PTR) record can be automatically created

Explanation: By creating the reverse-lookup zones in DNS Manager, the PTR records can be automatically created by checking a box.

74. Resolvers

Explanation: The client is responsible for generating the resolution request, which is then passed to the DNS server.

75. True

Explanation: DNS is not dynamically updated, so it is considered a static database.

76. IP address of DNS server

Explanation: The client needs the address of the DNS server configured in order to send it queries. It will not broadcast for DNS servers.

77. False

Explanation: The client needs the address of the DNS server configured in order to send it queries. It will not broadcast for DNS servers.

78. False

Explanation: The NetBIOS scope name has nothing to do with DNS.

Configuring HOSTS and LMHOSTS Files

79. False

Explanation: #DOM is only valid in LMHOSTS.

80. 163.84.56.6   Server4   #PRE   #DOM:GIANT

81. 130.10.4.5   SERVER1   NTSERVER   # test system

Explanation: The format of the HOSTS file is `IP-Address name alias #comment`.

82. Add the HOSTS file entries from the NT server to the Windows for Workgroups client machines.

Explanation: In a non-DNS environment, the HOSTS file is used to resolve name to IP addresses for non-NetBIOS systems.

83. 126.90.10.6   Server4   #PRE

#INCLUDE \\Server4\PUBLIC\LMHOSTS

Explanation: The #INCLUDE directive includes a centralized LMHOSTS file on the local system.

84. #BEGIN ALTERNATE, #END ALTERNATE

    Explanation: The ALTERNATE directives can be used to specify multiple servers in the LMHOSTS file.

85. #INCLUDE

    Explanation: This directive allows the use of a centralized LMHOSTS file to be included in a local host.

86. LMHOSTS

87. LMHOSTS

    Explanation: This file may be imported via WINS Manager to build static mappings.

88. #INCLUDE

    Explanation: This directive can be used to centrally locate an LMHOST file and load it on a local client.

89. #PRE

    Explanation: The #PRE directive preloads an entry in the LMHOSTS file into the NetBIOS cache.

90. True

    Explanation: If configured to do so, the HOSTS file can be used for NetBIOS name resolutions.

Setting Up TCP/IP Printing

91. LPR

    Explanation: The LPR utility causes a print job to execute on a remote system running the LPD service.

92. Either NetBEUI or TCP/IP will work.

Explanation: The client does not have to be using TCP/IP to send a job to the TCP/IP printer. The client sends the job to the Windows NT computer supplying TCP/IP print services, which then forwards the job to the TCP/IP printer.

93. Manual

94. False

Explanation: This version of TCP/IP Printing supports multiple data files per control file.

95. Either the printer's name or its IP address

96. Local (not share, if the two are different)

Configuring SNMP

97. In the SNMP Properties dialog box

98. True

Sample Test

2-1 B

Explanation: Wildcards can only be used for a complete octet.

2-2 B

Explanation: WINS does not significantly affect ARP, although it does significantly reduce broadcasts for name resolution.

2-3 B

2-4 B

Explanation: The DNS domain name can be configured in DHCP by option 15.

2-5 C

Explanation: Dhcprequests are sent if the client has been previously configured by DHCP. Dhcpdiscover is sent the first time the client initializes. The other options are server responses to the client.

2-6 D

Explanation: The HOSTS file was the original file used for name address resolution and is still used today in conjunction with other name address resolution techniques.

2-7 A

Explanation: The InterNIC is the authority that manages the DNS name space.

2-8 D

Explanation: The PTR record is used when you know the IP address of the host and need to find out the host name. It is always the IP address "backward" followed by `.in-addr.arpa`.

2-9 D

Explanation: This is what the `in-addr.arpa` file is used for and the purpose of the PTR record.

2-10 A

Explanation: A forwarder is designed to act as a single point of contact for all queries made for DNS servers that are external to the corporation.

2-11 B

Explanation: This is a Class B address subnetted on the third octet. The third octet must be equal to 30. The other choices are therefore on different subnets.

2-12 D

Explanation: Route Information Protocol (RIP) may be configured to exchange route information with other RIP configured routers in the network.

2-13 B

2-14 B

2-15 A, B, D

Explanation: There is no RESOLVER or SERVICE file. There is a SERVICES file, but this is not used for resolution.

2-16 B, E

Explanation: DNS is optional, WINS is optional, Scope ID is a NetBIOS option (not the same as a DHCP scope).

2-17 B

Explanation: Short lease times allow clients to give up their lease when roaming.

2-18 C

Explanation: It is always recommended to have primary and secondary WINS servers push/pull partners with each other.

2-19 B

2-20 B

Explanation: Default gateways are associated with the specific scope (segment) on which they reside.

2-21 A

Explanation: The global option is used to provide configuration parameters to the entire internetwork and, therefore, affects all scopes.

2-22 A, C

Explanation: Host name registration is not performed by DHCP. Administrator still needs to calculate subnets, which become DHCP scopes. DHCP does not replace DNS.

2-23 C

Explanation: 50% different might not provide enough addresses for one server to act as a primary and the other as a backup. You cannot configure multiple DHCP servers with the same IP addresses.

2-24 D

Explanation: BOOTP was the original protocol used in TCP/IP networks for automatically configuring TCP/IP clients. DHCP is derived from BOOTP.

2-25 C

2-26 C

Explanation: Route Information Protocol (RIP) uses the connectionless User Datagram Protocol (UDP) for transport. Transmission Control Protocol (TCP) is connection-oriented. The other choices are not transport layer protocols.

2-27 A, B, C, D, E

2-28 C

Explanation: This is a Class A IP address subnetted on the second octet. The network ID is 10.20.0.0. Other choices are on different networks.

2-29 C

Explanation: The LPR port is used in a Unix environment for TCP/IP printing.

2-30 B

2-31 B

Explanation: The #PRE directive preloads the names into the cache. Keeping them at the end of the file improves performance for looking up entries that are not in the cache, since they will be nearer the top of the LMHOSTS file.

2-32 B

Explanation: When a secondary server starts up, for example, it will request the primary's database. This update process is called a zone transfer and involves copying all the database files from the primary to the secondary.

Unit 3 Answers

Study Questions

Connecting to a Unix Host

1. TCP

   Explanation: Transmission Control Protocol (TCP) is the connection-oriented transport protocol. User Datagram Protocol (UDP) is connectionless.

2. `ftp`

3. `telnet`

4. False

   Explanation: Unix systems must run the LPD service.

5. Anonymous

6. False

   Explanation: As long as the particular hosts that they each need to communicate with are in their respective files, the HOSTS files on each system need not be the same.

7. True

   Explanation: The Windows NT system needs to address the printer directly without going through an intermediate system or spooler.

8. `telnet`

9. `ftp -s:ftpcmds sysux01`

   Explanation: The `-s` option specifies the script to use.

10. `finger julie fatboy`

11. False

    Explanation: The service on the Unix host must be running the `rsh` service. The `rcp` service does not exist.

12. `rcp`

13. False

    Explanation: The Trivial File Transfer Protocol (`tftp`) runs atop UDP, another connectionless protocol.

14. `rcp, rexec`

15. The RHOSTS file is a list of which remote users are allowed to run commands on the Unix host. Its format is similar to that of a HOSTS file.

16. `Telnet` is a terminal emulation utility that can be used to run interactive commands on the local host. Rsh can only run noninteractive commands.

17. `Get` and `put`. `Get` copies a file from the remote host to the local one, and `put` copies a file from the local host to the remote one.

18. Use the `-s: filename` switch with it, like `ftp -s: runonce`.

19. It lies in the type of security. `Rexec`'s use is password-protected, whereas `rhs`'s is verified by an RHOSTS file.

Configuring RAS and Dial-Up Networking With TCP/IP

20. True

    Explanation: Once the RAS client connects to the server, it behaves like any other machine on the network and can use DNS for host name resolution.

21. PPP

22. False

    Explanation: You can specify either the RAS server only or the entire network, but not a subset of the network.

23. You can provide a range of IP addresses for the RAS clients to be assigned when logging on.

24. False

    Explanation: The addresses should not match those used by DHCP server, as they may overlap.

25. False

    Explanation: You have the option of letting the server assign you an IP address, but not to connect to a specific DHCP server.

26. Name server

27. False

    Explanation: If TCP/IP is installed, any new connection will be set up to use it.

28. SLIP

29. RAS must be set so that outgoing calls can be made from the local computer.

Configuring Multiple-Domain Browsing in a Routed Network

30. Domain master browser

31. Master browser, backup browser, domain master browser

32. #DOM

Explanation: This directive points to the PDC in the domain.

33. True

34. False

Explanation: Some routers—not all—can be configured to permit NBT broadcasts to be forwarded after being sent to port 137.

35. WINS, LMHOSTS files, and use of a router's port 137

36. WINS

37. 15

38. This command is part of the LMHOSTS file on a master browser in a subnetted internetwork. The IP number is the IP address of the PDC that's the domain master browser, God-like is the NetBIOS name of the domain master browser for the Cassiopeia domain, and the name is preloaded into the name cache.

39. By using LMHOSTS files to locate the domain master browsers to the master browsers on each subnet

Sample Test

3-1 B

3-2 B, D

Explanation: Ftp is a reliable file transfer protocol, so it uses Transmission Control Protocol (TCP) for transport (rather than User Datagram Protocol, or UDP). Internet Protocol (IP) is the datagram delivery service at the network layer for TCP.

3-3 C

Explanation: The Microsoft client will print to a queue on the Windows NT system, which will then send the print job to the TCP/IP printer.

3-4   A

Explanation: The -s option causes a script to be executed.

3-5   B

Explanation: The -i option specifies no interaction.

3-6   B

3-7   B, D

3-8   A

Explanation: Although not all NT-Unix utilities require that you specify a remote host name, rsh does.

3-9   A

Explanation: Rcp can be run from a Windows NT machine to copy files from one Unix server to another. Rsh is a command to run services on a remote system.

3-10   C

Explanation: The address 197.45.3.0 is reserved, but you can use the rest of the block from x.x.x.1 to x.x.x.27.

Unit 4 Answers

Study Questions

Using SNMP

1.   SNMP management application

Explanation: Windows NT does not include SNMP management application capabilities, although the Windows NT Server Resource Kit does.

2. Trap

Explanation: The *trap* is the term used in SNMP management for sending an event or alarm status.

3. Simple Network Management Protocol

4. IP addresses or names of SNMP managers

Explanation: The client needs the IP address (or needs to resolve it) of the SNMP manager in order to send a trap to it.

5. Traps

Explanation: SNMP traps are events or alarms sent by an agent to the manager.

6. Internet

Explanation: The Internet Agent Service monitors IP information.

7. Authentication traps are sent to the management application specified in the SNMP Service Configuration

8. An SNMP request will be rejected if the community name in the request does not match the configured community name.

Explanation: The community names for agent and manager must match.

9. SNMP Security Configuration dialog box

10. WINS

11. SNMP

12. 1.3.6.1

Explanation: OIDs (object identifiers) are named not just by name but by category, and all SNMP OIDs are in the category identified by these numbers.

13. Node ID, OID, poll interval, and default log setting

14. SNMPUtil

    Explanation: SNMPUtil is a Resource Kit utility with which you can monitor MIBs on a specified machine.

15. DHCP, WINS, and IIS

16. False

    Explanation: Both are installed with SNMP, but the Trap service is set for manual startup.

17. Level, edge

18. Scope declaration, conditional statement(s)

    Explanation: The scope declaration identifies the node and OID to be monitored and logging conditions, and the conditional statement(s) define the events that will prompt logging.

19. 750ms, 2

    Explanation: These timeouts cannot be edited with SNMPMon.

20. True

21. This statement monitors object 1.3.6.1.51.14.2 at the node with the IP address 199.46.23.15 every two minutes, logging if a conditional statement is met.

22. `HKEY_LOCAL_MACHINE\SYSTEM\CurrentControlSet\Services\Tcpip\Parameters`

23. Contact, Location

    Explanation: These fields identify the SNMP administrator and where he or she is to be found.

24. Control

    Explanation: Simple Network Management Protocol (SNMP) may be used for both monitoring and controlling WINS servers.

25. Public

    Explanation: The community name public is the default and, therefore, widely known.

26. False

    Explanation: The agent can send the management station a trap directly without using the HOSTS file.

27. False

    Explanation: The agent can send the management station a trap directly without using the HOSTS file.

28. False

    Explanation: Both are case-sensitive.

29. HOSTS, DNS

    Explanation: SNMP may use HOSTS and DNS, but it is not required to use either. It may use IP addresses directly.

30. SNMP

    Explanation: Simple Network Management Protocol (SNMP) is used to manage and control devices on a TCP/IP network.

The Performance Monitor

31. Ping is running. Windows NT is sending a ping, but is not getting a reply.

    Explanation: ICMP echoes are ping messages.

32. True

    Explanation: This is one of many elements that Performance Monitor can track.

33. SNMP

    Explanation: Simple Network Management Protocol (SNMP) is a prerequisite for TCP/IP monitoring by Performance Monitor.

34. IP

    Explanation: Datagrams are associated with IP.

35. FTP

    Explanation: Logons are associated with FTP.

36. ICMP

37. IP

38. ICMP

    Explanation: Ping is ICMP echo.

39. TCP

    Explanation: Connections are associated with TCP.

40. TCP

41. FTP

    Explanation: Anonymous users are associated with FTP.

42. This category includes counters to monitor the rate at which bytes and packets are sent over a TCP/IP connection, the send and receive rates for TCP/IP segments, and the number of TCP/IP connections in each of the possible connection states.

43. Named, anonymous

44. It should remain constant or increase over time, as it records all attempted connections.

45. ICMP

46. False

Explanation: If a computer is set for IP routing, those packets are forwarded and counted as part of the datagrams forwarded/sec counter.

47. Datagrams

The Network Monitor

48. False

Explanation: A packet sent from a TCP/IP host to its own address will use the loopback interface and never be seen on the network.

49. Data stream

50. None

Explanation: For security reasons, Network Monitor will only capture packets for the computer on which it's running.

51. SAP

52. Filter

53. False

Explanation: Network Monitor can capture traffic sent either to or from the local server.

54. Disable all protocols and then enable the ones you want to monitor.

55. Hexadecimal

56. 14 bytes

The Event Viewer

57. Informational events, warning events, and error events

58. False

Explanation: Because TCP/IP is a protocol, not a service, the Event Viewer will not specifically mention it, but it will tell you that TCP/IP-related services did not start.

59. System

Explanation: The System log records events noted by Windows NT components such as services.

60. True

61. The Application log

62. Security, System, Application

Sample Test

4-1   B

Explanation: You need to specify both a transport protocol and a network protocol. SNMP uses UDP over IP. WINSOCK is not a transport protocol. TCP is not used with SNMP. ICMP is not a network layer protocol used for datagram delivery.

4-2   C

Explanation: Fragmentation is an IP datagram element. Fragmentation occurs when the Maximum Transmission Unit (MTU) of the router is smaller than the datagram and thus must be fragmented to pass through the network.

4-3   C

Explanation: Simple Network Management Protocol (SNMP) must be installed in order to use Performance Monitor with TCP/IP.

4-4   C

Explanation: Discarded Packets or Datagrams is a symptom of buffer space shortage

4-5   A

4-6   C

Explanation: Datagrams are associated with IP.

4-7   D

Explanation: Connections are associated with TCP.

4-8   TCP

Explanation: Connections are associated with TCP.

4-9   C

Explanation: Datagrams are associated with IP.

4-10   B

Explanation: Anonymous users are associated with FTP logons.

4-11   B

Explanation: Logons are associated with FTP.

4-12   B

Explanation: Performance Monitor uses SNMP to gather statistics for TCP/IP.

4-13   A

Explanation: Destination Unreachable is an ICMP message.

4-14 D

4-15 B

4-16 D

Explanation: Connections are associated with TCP.

4-17 C

Explanation: Datagrams are associated with IP.

4-18 A

Explanation: Echo is associated with ping (ICMP Echo).

4-19 B

4-20 A

Explanation: Ping is an ICMP protocol.

4-21 B

Explanation: IP is the routing protocol.

4-22 C

Explanation: Connections are associated with TCP.

4-23 B

Explanation: When an incorrect community name is used, the system will send a trap to the manager indicating that the SNMP packet was received and that authentication failed.

4-24 B

Explanation: Both the agent and the management station require the SNMP MIB.

4-25   C

Explanation: A trap is always sent to the trap destination entered for the SNMP configuration.

4-26   A

Explanation: The Management Information Base (MIB) stores the SNMP information about a system.

4-27   C

Explanation: Simple Network Management Protocol (SNMP) is a prerequisite for Performance Monitor in a TCP/IP network.

4-28   C

Explanation: These are the checkboxes in SNMP configuration. The Internet checkbox is the layer associated with IP routing.

4-29   B

Explanation: The community name is used for security and, like a password, must be the same on both the agent and the manager.

4-30   C

Explanation: If the named table is not found within the specified database, a new table is created, and the data logged there.

4-31   A, D

4-32   C

Explanation: If a monitored node description contains more than one conditional, only the first conditional met is logged. All others are ignored.

4-33   A

4-34   C

4-35   D

Unit 5 Answers

Study Questions

IP-Addressing Problems

1. TTL (Time To Live) is decreased by at least 1 second for every router the datagram traverses. When the TTL reaches zero, the datagram is discarded. This prevents datagrams from endlessly circling an internetwork.

2. False

3. If the two DHCP servers have scopes that overlap, they may each assign the same IP address.

4. Excluded

5. The subnet mask might be incorrect. If the subnet mask is wrong, John's subnet cannot be identified.

6. False

    Explanation: A single DHCP server would eliminate the problem of overlapping scopes, but if the DHCP server goes down, no one will be able to lease IP addresses. Instead, you should have two servers if possible, but be sure that their scopes don't overlap. Microsoft recommends splitting the scopes 25%–75% between DHCP servers.

Using TCP/IP Utilities to Resolve IP Configuration Problems

7. tracert

    Explanation: The tracert utility displays the time to travel through each router.

8. Duplicate IP address

   Explanation: This is an `arp` request sent when TCP initializes to determine if another host on the network has the same IP address.

9. ARP

10. `ipconfig /all`

    Explanation: The `ipconfig` utility displays all the relevant TCP/IP configuration information.

11. `nbtstat -R`

    Explanation: The `nbtstat -R` command loads name cache with entries in LMHOSTS file with #PRE directive. (You must use capital R to purge and reload; lowercase r lists names already resolved.)

12. Time to Live

13. `nbtstat`

    Explanation: The `nbtstat -c` command displays NetBIOS information. The `-c` option displays the cache information.

14. `ping`

15. PMTU discovery

    Explanation: Path Maximum Transmission Unit (PMTU) discovery uses Don Not Fragment so that the IP datagram won't be fragmented by a router with a small MTU. This causes `ping` to fail with an ICMP destination unreachable error message.

16. NETWORKS

    Explanation: The NETWORKS file performs resolution for network names in a similar way that the HOSTS file does for host names.

17. `arp -a`

    Explanation: The `arp -a` command displays the `arp` cache contents, which you can analyze for problems.

18. False

    Explanation: Static entries are unaffected by time interval but are deleted after rebooting.

19. DHCP

    Explanation: `/release` and `/renew` are commands to continue or end DHCP IP address leases.

20. TCP, UDP

21. ICMP

Name Resolution Problems

22. Broadcast

23. True

    Explanation: The hybrid (h-node) type of client will broadcast in an attempt to resolve names if other attempts have failed.

24. HOSTS

    Explanation: This file is used for host name resolution.

25. False

    Explanation: The secondary will be contacted only if the primary does not reply. If the primary replies either positively or negatively, the secondary will not be contacted.

26. Ping a remote host by name and IP address. If you can't get to it by name, you have a name problem. Also, if you can't resolve any names, ping the name resolution servers to make sure that they're up and running.

27. True

28. DHCP dynamically assigns IP addresses, whereas DNS maintains a static list of names mapped to IP addresses. If DHCP allocates addresses that have an entry in the DNS, the two hosts could conflict. Names assigned to DNS entries should be excluded from the DHCP pool.

29. DNS

Sample Test

5-1   B

5-2   C

5-3   A

Explanation: Loopback address is internal only.

5-4   B

Explanation: Since the ping must travel to a distant subnet, the route table is consulted to find the default gateway. The physical route the ping request must traverse is through the network interface on the default gateway. The arp utility is consulted to find the hardware address of the local network interface of the default gateway.

5-5   B

Explanation: Time to Live is the number of seconds that a datagram can exist on a network.

5-6   A

Explanation: This is displayed by the nbtstat -n command and shows the entry as <00>.

5-7   C

Explanation: This is displayed by the `nbtstat -n` command and shows the entry as <03>.

5-8   D

Explanation: This is displayed by the `nbtstat -n` command and shows the entry as <20>.

5-9   C

Unit 6 Answers

1.   D

Explanation: The HOSTS file was the original file used for name-address resolution and is still used today in conjunction with other name-address resolution techniques.

2.   B

3.   B

Explanation: A is invalid as it's a Class A address. B is a Class B address. C is invalid because it ends in zero and is therefore a network number, and D is invalid because 240 is within the range of experimental IP numbers, not the Class B range.

4.   B

Explanation: WINS does not significantly affect ARP, although it does significantly reduce broadcasts for name resolution by providing a centralized database to consult before resorting to broadcasts.

5.   B

6. E

Explanation: Subnets are not supported by bridging. You would need a router to subnet this network.

7. D

Explanation: The PTR record is used when you know the IP address of the host and need to find out the host name. It is always the IP address backward, followed by `.in-addr.arpa`.

8. D

9. E

Explanation: A forwarder is designed to act as a single point of contact for all queries made for DNS servers external to the corporation.

10. B, D

Explanation: `Ftp` is a reliable file transfer protocol, so it uses Transmission Control Protocol (TCP) for transport (rather than User Datagram Protocol, or UDP). Internet Protocol (IP) is the datagram delivery service at the network layer for TCP.

11. B, C

Explanation: Option A ends in zero and is therefore a network address. Option D ends in an invalid value, and option 3 is impossible to achieve with the specified subnet mask. B and C are both valid options. The operating system of the hosts is not relevant here.

12. D

Explanation: Route Information Protocol (RIP) may be configured to exchange route information with other RIP configured routers in the network.

13. B

Explanation: NBNS (NetBIOS Naming Service) is used to reconcile computer names with IP addresss. This is the function of WINS.

14. A

15. B

Explanation: Each scope defines the addresses that may be leased and those that are excluded from leasing for a subnet. If an address isn't defined in the scope, it's automatically excluded from the lease pool.

16. C

Explanation: It is always recommended to have primary and secondary WINS servers be push/pull partners with each other.

17. B

Explanation: Automatic updates between the partners are initiated by the push partner.

18. B

Explanation: Default gateways are associated with the specific scope (segment) on which they reside.

19. A, C

Explanation: Host name registration is not performed by DHCP. Administrator still needs to calculate subnets, which become DHCP scopes. DHCP does not replace HOSTS files.

20. C

Explanation: Discarded packets or datagrams are a symptom of buffer space shortage

21. C

Explanation: Microsoft recommends that each server keep a pool that's 75% local and a (separate) pool that's 25% on the other subnet, so that the other subnet will be supported even if it loses its DHCP server. These pools will all have to be distinct; you cannot configure multiple DHCP servers with the same IP addresses.

22. D

Explanation: BOOTP was the original protocol used in TCP/IP networks for automatically configuring TCP/IP clients. DHCP is derived from BOOTP.

23. C

24. B

Explanation: When an incorrect community name is used, the system will send a trap to the manager, indicating that the SNMP packet was received and that authentication failed.

25. C

Explanation: Route Information Protocol (RIP) uses the connectionless User Datagram Protocol (UDP) for transport. Transmission Control Protocol (TCP) is connection-oriented, and the other choices are not transport layer protocols.

26. B

27. B, C

28. C

29. B

30. B

Explanation: The #PRE directive preloads the names into the cache. Keeping them at the end of the file improves performance for looking up entries that are not in the cache, because they will be nearer the top of the LMHOSTS file.

31. B

Explanation: When a secondary server starts up, it will request the primary's database. This update process is called a zone transfer and involves copying all the database files from the primary to the secondary.

32. C

33. C

Explanation: The Microsoft client will print to a queue on the Windows NT system, which will then send the print job to the TCP/IP printer.

34. B

35. C

Explanation: Dhcprequests are sent if the client has been previously configured by DHCP. Dhcpdiscover is sent the first time the client initializes. The other options are server responses to the client.

36. A

Explanation: Although not all NT-Unix utilities require that you specify a remote host name, rsh does.

37. C

Explanation: The address 197.45.3.0 is reserved, but you can use the rest of the block from x.x.x.1 to x.x.x.26.

38. B

Explanation: You need to specify both a transport protocol and a network protocol. SNMP uses UDP over IP. WINSOCK is not a transport protocol. TCP is not used with SNMP. ICMP is not a network layer protocol used for datagram delivery.

39. C

Explanation: Fragmentation occurs when the Maximum Transmission Unit (MTU) of the router is smaller than the datagram and thus must be fragmented to pass through the network. If you specify that a datagram is not to be fragmented, the operation may fail.

40. C

Explanation: Simple Network Management Protocol (SNMP) must be installed in order to use Performance Monitor with TCP/IP.

41. D

Explanation: Connections are associated with TCP, which is a connection-oriented transport protocol.

42. B

Explanation: The -i option specifies no interaction.

43. A

Explanation: ICMP is the protocol used to send ping messages, with which you can determine that the destination is unreachable.

44. A

Explanation: Echo is associated with ping (ICMP Echo).

45. B

46. C

47. B

Explanation: Object MIBS must be present on both the agent and the management station.

48. C

Explanation: A trap is always sent to the trap destination entered for the SNMP configuration.

49. C

Explanation: Simple Network Management Protocol (SNMP) is a prerequisite for Performance Monitor in a TCP/IP network.

50. B

Explanation: The community name is used for security and, like a password, must be the same on both the agent and the manager.

51. B

52. B

Explanation: 224 in decimal is 11100000 in binary. The three 1s provide 8 subnets (2 to the third power is 8). Two of these are unusable—the base subnet and the broadcast. This yields 8-2=6 usable subnets. Other combinations yield more than 6 subnets and produce fewer hosts per subnet.

53. A

Explanation: The -s option causes a script to be executed.

54. B

Explanation: The DNS domain name can be configured in DHCP by option 15.

55. B

Explanation: Performance Monitor uses SNMP to gather statistics for TCP/IP.

56. B, D

57. A

Explanation: ping runs on ICMP.

58. B

Explanation: DNS and WINS are optional; scope ID is not needed.

59. A

Explanation: WINS is the only Windows NT service that contains manageable objects.

60. B, D

61. C

Explanation: If the named table is not found within the specified database, a new table is created and the data logged there.

62. A, C, D

63. D

64. C

Explanation: If a monitored node description contains more than one conditional, only the first conditional met is logged. All others are ignored.

65. B

Explanation: The first statement would only record it if the toast were burned at level 8, but not at 9 or 10. The third uses invalid syntax (and would record underdone toast anyway). Only B will log the event when the value of toastDoneness exceeds 7.

66. B

Explanation: Short lease times allow clients to give up their leases when roaming.

67. B

68. D

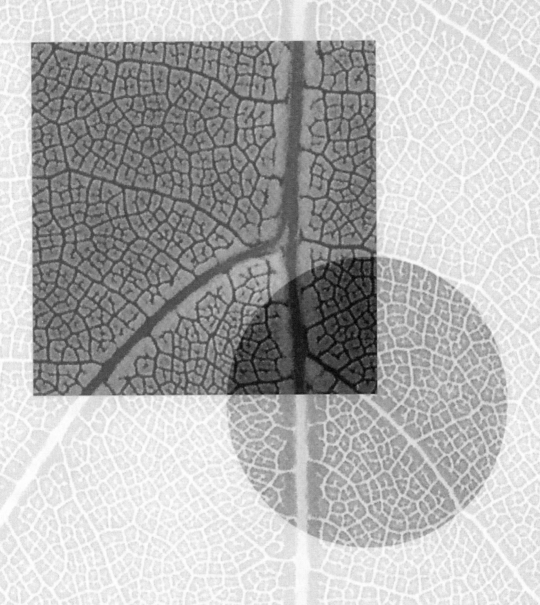

Glossary

Address   In TCP/IP, an IP address is a 32-bit numeric identifier assigned to a node. The address has two parts, one for the network identifier and the other for the node identifier. All nodes on the same network must share the network address and have a unique node address. For networks connected to the Internet, network addresses are assigned by the Internet Activities Board (IAB).

Addresses also include IPX addresses—the internal network number and external network number—and the MAC (Media Access Control) address assigned to each network card or device.

Advanced Research Projects Agency Network (ARPANET)   A packet-switched network developed in the early 1970s for communication among research organizations. The "father" of today's Internet. ARPANET was decommissioned in June 1990.

Agents   In the client/server model, the part of the system that performs information preparation and exchange on behalf of a client or server application.

Application Layer   The layer of the OSI model that interfaces with user mode applications by providing high-level network services based upon lower-level network layers. Network file systems like named pipes are an example of Application layer software. See *Open System Interconnection*.

Application Program Interface (API)   A set of routines that an application program uses to request and carry out lower-layer services performed by the operating system.

ARP (Address Resolution Protocol)   IP address to hardware address translation protocol.

Asynchronous Data Transmission   A type of communication that sends data using flow control rather than a clock to synchronize data between the source and destination.

Bandwidth   In network communications, the amount of data that can be sent across a wire in a given time. Each communication that passes along the wire decreases the amount of available bandwidth.

Binary   The numbering system used in computer memory and in digital communication. All characters are represented as a series of 1s and 0s. For example, the letter *A* might be represented as 01000001.

Binding   A process that establishes the initial communication channel between the protocol driver and the network adapter card driver.

Bits   In binary data, each unit of data is a bit. Each bit is represented by either 0 or 1 and is stored in memory as an ON or OFF state.

Boot Partition   The volume, formatted for either an NTFS or FAT file system, that contains the Windows NT operating system's files. Windows NT automatically creates the correct configuration and checks this information whenever you start your system.

Bridge   A device that connects two segments of a network and sends data to one or the other based on a set of criteria.

Buffers   A reserved portion of memory in which data is temporarily held pending an opportunity to complete its transfer to or from a storage device or another location in memory.

Circuit Switching   A type of communication system that establishes a connection, or circuit, between the two devices before communicating and does not disconnect until all data is sent.

Client   Clients run client software to provide network access. A piece of software that accesses data on a server can also be called a client.

Communication Protocol   For computers engaged in telecommunications, the protocol (i.e., the settings and standards) must be the same for both devices when receiving and transmitting information. A communications program can be used to ensure that the baud rate, duplex, parity, data bits, and stop bits are correctly set.

Connectionless   The model of interconnection in which communication takes place without first establishing a connection. Sometimes called datagram. IP and UDP are the two connectionless protocols in the TCP/IP suite.

Connection-Oriented   The model of interconnection in which communication proceeds through three well-defined phases: connection establishment, data transfer, connection releases. TCP is an example of a connection-oriented protocol.

Daemon   A utility program that runs on a TCP/IP server. Daemon programs run in the background, performing services such as file transfers, printing, calculations, searching for information, and many other tasks. This is similar to a TSR program in DOS. Daemons are fully supported by Unix, however.

DARPA (Defense Advanced Research Projects Agency)   The U.S. government agency that funded the ARPANET.

Data Frames   Logical, structured packets in which data can be placed. The Data Link layer packages raw bits from the Physical layer into data frames. The exact format of the frame used by the network depends on the topology.

Data Link Layer   The OSI layer that is responsible for data transfer across a single physical connection, or series of bridged connections, between two network entities.

Data Packet   A unit of data being sent over a network. A packet includes a header, addressing information, and the data itself. A packet is treated as a single unit as it is sent from device to device.

Data Transfer Rate   The data transfer rate determines how fast a drive or other peripheral can transfer data with its controller. The data transfer rate is a key measurement in drive performance.

Datagram   A packet of information and associated delivery information, such as the destination address, that is routed through a packet-switching network.

Dedicated Line   A transmission medium that is used exclusively between two locations. Dedicated lines are also known as leased lines or private lines.

Default Gateway   IP uses the default gateway address when it cannot find the destination host on the local subnet. This is usually the router interface.

Device Driver   A piece of software that allows an operating system to communicate with a hardware device. For example, disk drivers are used to control disk drives, and network drivers are used to communicate with network boards.

DHCP (Dynamic Host Configuration Protocol)   A method of automatically assigning IP addresses to client computers on a network.

Domain   The segment of the Internet to which a server belongs. There are six general domain names: .com (commercial enterprises), .edu (educational institutions), .org (nonprofit organizations), .gov (government), .mil (military installations), and .net (general domain).

Domain Name   The full name of a server to identify it on the Internet. Within the six main domains, organizations can request names of their own, such as whitehouse.gov (identifying *which* server in the .gov domain is being referred to). Domain names can be nested if necessary.

DNS   (1) Domain Name Service, the Windows NT service used to map IP addresses to domain names. (2) Domain Name System, the distributed name/address mechanism used in the Internet.

Dumb Terminal   A workstation consisting of keyboard and monitor, used to put data into the computer or receive information from the computer. Dumb terminals were originally developed to be connected to computers running a multi-user operating system so that users could communicate directly with them. All processing is done at and by the computer, not the dumb terminal. In contrast, a smart terminal contains processing circuits that can receive data from the host computer and later carry out independent processing operations.

Error Control   An arrangement that combines error detection and error correction.

Error Correction   A method used to correct erroneous data produced during data transmission, transfer, or storage.

File Transfer Protocol (FTP)   A TCP/IP protocol that permits the transferring of files between computer systems. Because FTP has been implemented on numerous types of computer systems, file transfers can be done between disparate computer systems.

Frame   A data structure that network hardware devices use to transmit data between computers. Frames consist of the addresses of the sending and receiving computers, size information, and a checksum. Frames are envelopes around packets of data that allow them to be addressed to specific computers on a shared media network.

FTP   See *File Transfer Protocol*.

Full-Duplex   A method of transmitting information over an asynchronous communications channel, in which signals may be sent in both directions simultaneously. This technique makes the best use of line time but substantially increases the amount of logic required in the primary and secondary stations.

Gateway   In TCP/IP terms, the computer connecting two distinct networks, such as the computer connecting a LAN to the Internet. May also refer to a router connecting subnets.

Gopher   An Internet tool that organizes topics into a menu system that users can employ to find information. Gopher also transparently connects users with the Internet server on which the information resides.

Half-Duplex   A method of transmitting information over a communication channel, in which signals may be sent in both directions, but only one way at a time. This is sometimes referred to as local echo.

Handshaking   In network communication, a process used to verify that a connection has been established correctly. Devices send signals back and forth to establish parameters for communication.

Hardware Address   See *Media Access Control (MAC) Address.*

Hop   Transferring a packet from router to router.

Hop Count   The number of routers a message must pass through to reach its destination. A hop count may be used to determine the most efficient network route.

Host   An addressable node on a TCP/IP network. Examples include end-point systems such as workstations, servers, minicomputers, and mainframes and immediate systems such as routers.

HOSTS Table   A table used to map IP addresses to domain names. Used if the Domain Name Service is not available.

ICMP (Internet Control Message Protocol)   A protocol at the Internet layer of the DoD model that sends messages between routers and other devices, letting them know of congested routes.

IGP (Interior Gateway Protocol)   The protocol used to exchange routing information between collaborating routers in the Internet. RIP and OSPF are examples of IGPs.

Internet   A global network made up of a large number of individual networks interconnected through the use of TCP/IP protocols. The individual networks that make up the Internet are from colleges, universities, businesses, research organizations, government agencies, individuals, and other bodies. The governing body of this global network is the Internet Activities Board (IAB). When the term *Internet* is used with an uppercase *I*, it refers to the global network, but with a lowercase *i*, it simply means a group of interconnected networks.

Internet Address   A 32-bit value displayed in numbers that specifies a particular network and a particular node on that network.

Internet Protocol (IP)   The Network layer protocol upon which the Internet is based. IP provides a simple connectionless packet exchange. IP cooperates with TCP (a connection-oriented protocol) to guarantee packet delivery. See *Internet*.

IP Address   A 32-bit (4-byte) number that uniquely identifies a computer on an IP internetwork. InterNIC assigns the first bytes of Internet IP addresses and administers them in hierarchies. In a Class A address, InterNIC assigns the first byte, and the owning organization assigns the remaining three bytes. In a Class B address, InterNIC or the higher level ISP assigns the first two bytes, and the organization assigns the remaining two bytes. In a Class C address, InterNIC or the higher level ISP assigns the first three bytes, and the organization assigns the remaining byte. Organizations not attached to the Internet can assign IP addresses as they please. See *Internet Protocol, Internet*.

LMHOSTS Table   A table used to map IP addresses to NetBIOS names. Used with the Windows Internet Name Service.

Management Information Base (MIB)   The entire set of objects that any service or protocol uses in SNMP. Because different network-management services are used for different types of devices or for different network-management protocols, each service has its own set of objects.

Map   To translate one value into another.

Master Browser   The computer on a network that maintains a list of computers and services available on the network and distributes the list to other browsers.

Media Access Control (MAC) Address   Hardware address burned into the Network Interface cards. Six bytes long, three given to the manufacture from the IEEE, and three bytes designated by the manufacturer.

Multihomed Host   A computer connected to more than one physical data link. The data links may or may not be attached to the same network.

Multilink   A capability of RAS to combine multiple data streams into one network connection for the purpose of using more than one modem or ISDN channel in a single connection. This feature is new to Windows NT 4.0.

NetBEUI   NetBIOS Extended User Interface. The primary local area network transport protocol in Windows NT. A simple Network layer transport developed to support NetBIOS installations. NetBEUI is not routable, and so it is not appropriate for larger networks. NetBEUI is the fastest transport protocol available for Windows NT.

NetBIOS (Network Basic Input/Output System)   A client/server interprocess communication service developed by IBM in the early 1980s. NetBIOS presents a relatively primitive mechanism for communication in client/server applications, but its widespread acceptance and availability across most operating systems makes it a logical choice for simple network applications. Many Windows NT network IPC mechanisms are implemented over NetBIOS.

NetBIOS over TCP/IP (NetBT)   A network service that implements the NetBIOS IPC over the TCP/IP protocol stack. See *NetBEUI.*

Network Layer   The layer of the OSI model that creates a communication path between two computers via routed packets. Transport protocols implement both the Network layer and the Transport layer of the OSI stack. IP is a Network layer service.

Node   In TCP/IP, an IP addressable computer system, such as workstations, servers, minicomputers, mainframes, and routers. In IPX networks, the term is usually applied to nonserver devices: workstations and printers.

Open System Interconnection (OSI)   A model defined by the ISO to conceptually organize the process of communication between computers in terms of seven layers, called protocol stacks. The seven layers of the OSI model helps you to understand how communication across various protocols takes place.

OSPF (Open Shortest Path First)   A proposed routing standard, IGP for the Internet.

OSI   See *Open System Interconnection.*

Packet   The basic division of data sent over a network. Each packet contains a set amount of data along with a header, containing information about the type of packet and the network address to which it is being sent. The size and format of packets depends on the protocol and frame types used.

Packet Switching   A type of data transmission in which data is divided into packets, each of which has a destination address. Each packet is then routed across a network in an optimal fashion. An addressed packet may travel a different route than packets related to it. Packet sequence numbers are used at the destination node to reassemble related packets.

Physical Layer   The physical components of a network.

Ping (Packet Internet Groper)   A packet used to test reachability of destinations by sending them an ICMP echo request and waiting for a reply. The term is used as a verb: "Ping host A to see if it is up."

PPP (Point-to-Point Protocol)   This protocol allows the sending of IP packets on a dial-up (serial) connection. Supports compression and IP address negotiation.

Presentation Layer   The layer of the OSI model that converts and translates (if necessary) information between the Session and Application layers.

Protocol Suite   A collection of protocols that are associated with and that implement a particular communication model (such as the TCP/IP protocol suite).

RIP (Routing Information Protocol)   A distance-vector routing protocol used on many TCP/IP internetworks and IPX networks. The distance vector algorithm uses a "fewest-hops" routing calculation method.

Router   (A) A device that connects two dissimilar networks and allows packets to be transmitted and received between them. (B) A connection between two networks that specifies message paths and may perform other functions, such as data compression.

Serial   A method of communication that transfers data across a medium one bit at a time, usually adding stop, start, and check bits to ensure quality transfer.

SLIP (Serial Line Internet Protocol)   A protocol that permits the sending of IP packets on a dial-up (serial) connection. SLIP does not support compression or IP address negotiation by itself.

Session Layer   The layer of the OSI model dedicated to maintaining a bidirectional communication connection between two computers. The Session layer uses the services of the Transport layer to provide this service.

Simple Network Management Protocol (SNMP)   A management protocol used on many networks, particularly TCP/IP. It defines the type, format, and retrieval of node management information.

Simplex   Data transmission in one direction only.

Start Bit   A bit that is sent as part of a serial communication stream to signal the beginning of a byte or packet.

Stop Bit   A bit that is sent as part of a serial communication stream to signal the end of a byte or packet.

Subnet Mask   Under TCP/IP, 32-bit values that allow a router to determine which subnet (subdivision of a network) an IP address is on.

Synchronous   Pertaining to two or more processes that depend upon the occurrence of a specific event, such as a common timing signal.

TCP (Transport Layer Protocol)   Implements guaranteed packet delivery using the Internet Protocol (IP).

Telnet   A TCP/IP terminal emulation protocol that permits a node, called the Telnet client, to log in to a remote node, called the Telnet server. The client simply acts as a dumb terminal, displaying output from the server. The processing is done at the server.

Terminal Emulation   The process of emulating a terminal, or allowing a PC to act as a terminal for a mainframe or Unix system.

Transport Layer   The OSI model layer responsible for the guaranteed serial delivery of packets between two computers over an internetwork. TCP is the Transport Layer Protocol for the TCP/IP transport protocol.

Transport Protocol   A service that delivers discrete packets of information between any two computers in a network. Higher level connection-oriented services are built upon transport protocols.

UDP (User Datagram Protocol)   A connectionless network packet protocol implemented on IP that is far faster than TCP because it doesn't have flow-control overhead. UDP can be implemented as a reliable transport when some higher-level protocol (such as NetBIOS) exists to make sure that required data eventually will be retransmitted in local area environments.

Universal Naming Convention (UNC)   A multivendor, multiplatform convention for identifying shared resources on a network.

Windows Internet Name Service (WINS)   A network service for Microsoft networks that provides Windows computers with Internet numbers for specified NetBIOS names, facilitating browsing and intercommunication over TCP/IP networks.

Index

Note to the Reader: Throughout this index **boldfaced** page numbers indicate primary discussions of a topic. *Italicized* page numbers indicate illustrations.

MCSE CORE REQUIREMENT STUDY GUIDES FROM NETWORK PRESS

Sybex's Network Press presents updated and expanded second editions of the definitive study guides for MCSE candidates.

MCSE: NETWORKING ESSENTIALS Study Guide SECOND EDITION

EXAM 70-058

JAMES CHELLIS
CHARLES PERKINS
MATTHEW STREBE

ISBN: 0-7821-2220-5
704pp; 7¹/₂" x 9"; Hardcover
$49.99

MCSE: NT WORKSTATION 4 Study Guide SECOND EDITION

EXAM 70-073

CHARLES PERKINS
MATTHEW STREBE
AND JAMES CHELLIS

ISBN: 0-7821-2223-X
784pp; 7¹/₂" x 9"; Hardcover
$49.99

MCSE: NT SERVER 4 Study Guide SECOND EDITION

EXAM 70-067

MATTHEW STREBE
CHARLES PERKINS
WITH JAMES CHELLIS

ISBN: 0-7821-2222-1
832pp; 7¹/₂" x 9"; Hardcover
$49.99

MCSE: NT SERVER 4 IN THE ENTERPRISE Study Guide SECOND EDITION

EXAM 70-068

LISA DONALD
WITH JAMES CHELLIS

ISBN: 0-7821-2221-3
704pp; 7¹/₂" x 9"; Hardcover
$49.99

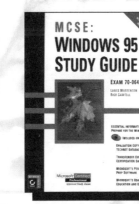

MCSE: WINDOWS 95 STUDY GUIDE

EXAM 70-064

LANCE MORTENSEN
RICK SAWTELL

ISBN: 0-7821-2256-6
800pp; 7¹/₂" x 9"; Hardcover
$49.99

A $50.00 SAVINGS!

MCSE Core Requirements
Box Set
ISBN: 0-7821-2245-0
4 hardcover books;
3,024pp total; $149.96

Microsoft Certified Professional — *Approved Study Guide*

NETWORK PRESS SYBEX®

STUDY GUIDES FOR THE MICROSOFT CERTIFIED SYSTEMS ENGINEER EXAMS

MCSE ELECTIVE STUDY GUIDES FROM NETWORK PRESS®

Sybex's Network Press expands the definitive study guide series for MCSE candidate

MCSE: TCP/IP FOR NT SERVER 4 STUDY GUIDE THIRD EDITION

EXAM 70-059

TODD LAMMLE WITH MONICA LAMMLE AND JAMES CHELLIS

ISBN: 0-7821-2224-8
688pp; 7 1/2" x 9"; Hardcover
$49.99

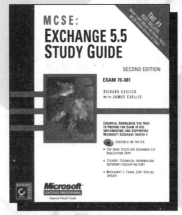

MCSE: EXCHANGE 5.5 STUDY GUIDE SECOND EDITION

EXAM 70-081

RICHARD EASLICK WITH JAMES CHELLIS

ISBN: 0-7821-2261-2
848pp; 7 1/2" x 9"; Hardcover
$49.99

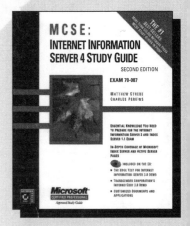

MCSE: INTERNET INFORMATION SERVER 4 STUDY GUIDE SECOND EDITION

EXAM 70-087

MATTHEW STREBE CHARLES PERKINS

ISBN: 0-7821-2248-5
704pp; 7 1/2" x 9"; Hardcover
$49.99

MCSE: SQL SERVER 6.5 ADMINISTRATION STUDY GUIDE

LANCE MORTENSEN RICK SAWTELL MICHAEL LEE

ISBN: 0-7821-2172-1
672pp; 7 1/2" x 9"; Hardcover
$49.99

MCSE: PROXY SERVER 2 Study Guide

EXAM 70-088

ERIK ROZELL AND TODD LAMMLE WITH JAMES CHELLIS

ISBN: 0-7821-2194-2
576pp; 7 1/2" x 9"; Hardcover
$49.99

MCSE: EXCHANGE 5 STUDY GUIDE

RICHARD EASLICK WITH JAMES CHELLIS

ISBN: 0-7821-1967-0
656pp; 7 1/2" x 9"; Hardcover
$49.99

Microsoft® Certified **Professional**
Approved Study Guide

NETWORK PRESS® SYBEX

STUDY GUIDES FOR THE MICROSOFT CERTIFIED SYSTEMS ENGINEER EXAMS